SOLICITORS
to SCOTLAND

SOLICITORS *to* SCOTLAND

SEDUCTION, SEDITION AND SUBTERFUGE IN THE LOST HISTORY OF A LAW FIRM

Ewan McCall

ORIGIN

First published in Great Britain in 2022 by
John Donald, an imprint of Birlinn Ltd

West Newington House
10 Newington Road
Edinburgh
EH9 1QS

www.birlinn.co.uk

ISBN: 978 1 83983 025 9

The publishers gratefully acknowledge the support of

towards the publication of this book

British Library Cataloguing-in-Publication Data
A catalogue record for this book is available on request
from the British Library

Typeset by Initial Typesetting Services, Edinburgh

Printed and bound in Britain by Clays Ltd, Elcograf S.p.A.

Contents

Acknowledgements

In researching and writing this book I had the great experience of speaking to people from across the world and I am enormously grateful to all of them.

I was first encouraged to pursue this research at the University of St Andrews, by Dr Ana Del Campo, a medieval historian who strikes a mix of fear and love into the heart of every student and is unrivalled in her dedication to them. I would also like to thank Dr Chandrika Kaul, whose enthusiasm and extensive knowledge of Indian history inspired me to piece together the story of Alexander Duncan, and Professor Colin Kidd who gave me the confidence to elevate this story from several pages to several chapters. Without the assistance of Professor John Cairns of the University of Edinburgh, who helped me cultivate a previously non-existent knowledge of Scots Law, this book would have been considerably shorter.

Further afield, Robert Alloo and the Bruce family both provided invaluable family accounts of their ancestors, John Gibson and Jamima Beck respectively, which helped bring the individuals to life, recounting a fascinating tale in the process. James Hamilton of the Society of Writers to Her Majesty's Signet was also incredibly helpful in helping me better understand how the lawyers of Anderson Strathern fit into legal society at large, as were Jack Reid of Tain Parish Church and Margaret Urquhart of Tain Museum, who helped me piece together the life of Rosemary Mackenzie. Euan Notley's keen eye for detail also proved invaluable throughout the writing process and I am very grateful for his time. The support and enthusiasm of those around me, especially my family and my partner Nick, is hugely appreciated.

My greatest thanks go to everyone at Anderson Strathern for their emotive and knowledgeable assistance when I was writing this history. In particular, I would like to thank Robert Soper and Stuart Gibb for their help in uncovering the hidden treasures of a twenty-first-century office, Catriona Watt and Beth Cameron for giving me the encouragement to make this book a reality, Frazor Murphy for capturing the discoveries on camera and Adrian Smith for motivating me with determination and skill to get the project to the finishing line. To Nigel Buchanan, Andrew Kerr, Alan Masson, George Russell and Douglas Stewart I am also hugely grateful for animated conversations about their trials and tribulations, past and present.

List of Plates

1. Copy of a Heritable Bond from the reign of James IV, written in Scots (1505).

2. Letter from Edward, Earl of Conway, concerning the Court of Charles II (1681).

3. Dispensation and Assignation from Adam Smith to Robert Balfour Ramsay (1754).

4. Legitimisation of Charlotte Stewart under the Privy Seal of George III (1796).

5. Portrait of John Davidson in conversation with Lord Henderland, George Paton, Lord Monboddo and James Hutton.

6. John Gibson in old age (c. 1870).

7. Letter books of Alexander Stevenson Blair (1889–1913).

8. Cartoon titled 'Lambast of Muir', with Muir (unknown) being hung by representations of justice, virtue, education etc. (nineteenth century).

9. Ian Mackenzie, partner at Strathern & Blair, in Djerba, Tunisia, during the North African Campaign (c. 1942).

10. Rosemary Mackenzie, secretary at Strathern & Blair, around her time in Italy with the British Army (c. 1944).

11. J&F Anderson retirement party for Pat Smyth (1968).

12. J&F Anderson Coat of Arms (1990), detailing the history of J&F Anderson from its founding by Thomas Cranstoun in the eighteenth century.

Abbreviations

AS	Anderson Strathern
EIC	East India Company
NA	National Archives
NLS	National Library of Scotland
NRS	National Records of Scotland
NTS	National Trust for Scotland
RAF	Royal Air Force
RSE	Royal Society of Edinburgh
SPCK	Society for the Propagation of Christian Knowledge
SSC	Society of Solicitors to the Supreme Courts of Scotland
WAAF	Women's Auxiliary Air Force
WS	Writer to the Signet
YWCA	Young Women's Christian Association

PART 1

TRIALS AND TRIBULATIONS FROM THE ARCHIVES

Introduction

The chests remained shut. With each whack of the locksmith's mallet, another ancient mechanism slid into place, but the huge iron boxes refused to open. Agitation was beginning to show among the assembled guests, many of whom had been patiently waiting for over an hour to see what these old relics might contain. Never work with animals, children or sixteenth-century cast-iron Nuremberg chests. But, finally, there was some hope. The locksmith indicated that one of the chests was on the verge of opening; the onlookers stood on their toes in hope of catching the first glance of items entombed for over a hundred years. The lid swung open, and we all looked inside.

Nothing. Well, not quite nothing – at the bottom of the chest was the accumulated debris of one hundred years' worth of rubbish jammed through a narrow keyhole: cigarette butts, paperclips, wrappers. With the second chest moments away from being opened, the prospect of discovery had been halved, as had the expectations of the now fidgety solicitors. But just as the romantic mystery of these objects seemed to fade, along with the stories they might tell, their story was wrestled back in full technicolour as the second chest fell open, revealing an interior brimming with letters, diaries, wills and writs, all covered in a thick layer of coal dust.

Legal histories are not typically a stage for mystery, tragedy, romance or blasphemy. As a directory of achievements and precedents they can be useful, but as a repository for the stories of people, and of ideas, they generally fall flat on their face. In this book you will not find chapters devoted to the arrival of the fax machine. Instead, this is the story of how people, connected by the common thread of the law, helped shape modern Scotland in the company of philosophers, inventors, writers and rogues. As the centuries progress, the people's faces and backgrounds become more varied and diverse as each generation contends with a society in conflict with itself. The top hats come off, the trench boots come on, and women finally break through into a profession previously dominated by men.

At first glance you might think that the story of Anderson Strathern, the law firm to which the chests belong, is a short one. Based in modern-looking offices in Edinburgh, Glasgow and elsewhere, it provides legal services across a variety of sectors, old and new. Nevertheless, the modern law firm is the product of roughly a dozen historical practices through which Scotland's legal journey can be traced – including J&F Anderson, Strathern and Blair, and Bell and Scott – stretching from monastic scribes to the modern lawyer. We will treat their stories as a unified whole, connected in context, scale and practice. In some cases, these historical legal practices also overlap, exchanging apprentices and letters until they finally converge in the twentieth and twenty-first centuries. From the vantage point of the present, just as with a family, they are all branches of the same tree.

It is a perilous task weaving a common thread through the facts, anecdotes and legalese these practices left behind. The same can be said of Scotland's own history. At least some of the first individuals to seriously document Scotland's history thought so, with David Hume giving up on his 'History of Great Britain' in favour of a 'History of England' as he saw no clear chain of events running from Scotland's supposedly feudal and despotic past to its enlightened and commercial present. With hindsight, Hume may have taken a different view. The Enlightenment of which he was a fundamental part was no accident, and was partially based on pioneering universities, a strong mercantile tradition, an independent legal system and the world's first system of universal education. Their combination led to an explosion of creativity, originality and intellectual fervour that these practices not only embraced but contributed towards. Even today, the Enlightenment values of reason, individualism and moral sense hold an important place in the proper functioning of the law.

Most modern histories have, at least in part, been put together using information from earlier books and memoirs. In this book, we are confronted with a huge array of new material never before analysed, often dealing with characters and incidents so obscure they have fallen between the cracks of larger works – the footnotes of history. Much of this history is based on information gathered from material unearthed from one of three ancient iron chests. Almost as much unarchived, unknown material was also found elsewhere in these modern offices, in old boxes and quiet corners. Together, these forgotten documents form an intricate trail leading to unusual, powerful and bizarre stories. In the chapters of this book, we resurrect the lost individuals at the heart of these stories, locked, until now, within three iron chests. The documents include the machinations of nobles at the court of Charles II, a blood-stained search warrant for a Jacobite ship, a lost legal case brought to the Court of Session by Adam Smith, panicked discussions of the financial ruin of Sir Walter Scott, counter-reformation papal decrees, charters from Robert the Bruce and Georgian letters between India and Scotland detailing a tragedy fuelled by lies, sex and murder. This may be only the tip of the iceberg, an iceberg that descends deep into the obscure recesses of archives across the country. In the National Records of Scotland (NRS) alone, possibly more than a hundred thousand pages of historical documentation pertaining to these stories remain waiting to be read. No doubt their

One of three iron Nuremberg chests reopened in 2019,
with swan details in the lid.

contents would reveal secrets about Scotland's story that would
dwarf the short stories told here.

Now it is time to delve into the contents of these long-
forgotten chests and to reimagine the lives, times and work
of the people who brushed shoulders with kings and popes,
Hume and Smith, Burns and Scott, prime ministers and prime
suspects.

The Nuremburg Chests, c. 1550–1706

These large sixteenth-century Nuremburg chests, commonly known as Armada chests, were once used to store important documentation on behalf of clients. They are substantial iron boxes with an intricate locking mechanism, impervious to fire and being bashed about: the ideal insurance policy. Despite the advances since their creation, opening these chests was a considerable challenge in the absence of a key. Wherever Anderson Strathern's predecessors have moved over the past few hundred years, the three chests have moved with them.

Until 2019, the three chests had been locked for several generations. One former partner, who first apprenticed at Strathern & Blair in the 1940s, recounted that even then no one had seen them open. With the help of a master locksmith, the chests' lids were gradually prised open until instruments could be inserted into the lock mechanism. Having gained access without damage to the antique metalwork, we could see that the physical interiors of the chests were as intriguing as the external cases. In one, the lock mechanism was covered in a grate of intricately worked metal mermaids, another bore the sigil of an early Edinburgh guild, another a painting of a swan gliding on a body of water. Inside the chests, coated in a thick layer of coal dust, we uncovered a hoard of material from early modern times to the eve of the First World War. It is from these documents, and a multitude of unpublished documents found in their vicinity, that the majority of this book is composed.

1

The Distant Past

'The name and estimatioun of ane advocate is becum
vyle . . . '

On sheets of stiff and yellowed vellum, inscribed with faint
Latin writs, we find the earliest links between the solicitors of
today and a distant past. The lawyers who created or held these
documents are not partners in the modern sense, but are connected to the present through the older tradition of transfer of
clients, documents and knowledge from master to apprentice.
In the case of Anderson Strathern, this tradition, stretching far
beyond the earliest verifiable partners of the early eighteenth
century, has conferred the vestiges of a medieval origin – with
archives teeming with the trials and tribulations of peasants,
kings and popes. Known by the Scots term 'Writer', these early
lawyers lived through the dying days of the Middle Ages, as
Scottish monarchs of limited authority holed themselves up
in palatial fortresses, justifiably wary of the schemes of envious
clan chiefs and nobles. But it was not in these great castles,
or on the battlefield, that the initial foundations of a written,
distinctly Scottish law were laid. Its origin, and that of the legal
profession, lie in the centuries following the end of Roman
rule in Britain, well beyond the sights of any documented legal
lineage but vital in understanding what followed. Our story
begins in the seventh century.

To those north of the ruinous Hadrian's Wall, the Roman
presence was a distant memory. Although the political influence

of the Empire enjoyed an unusually long afterlife, a gradual re-organisation of society was underway with Britain divided into smaller political units and undergoing several waves of immigration from continental Europe. The embryonic Scotland of the seventh century was loosely divided into disparate groups of people – Picts, Gaels, Angles and Britons – and the law for these people was often fluid and unwritten. Most individuals did not travel more than a few miles from their birthplace throughout their lives, so the administrative simplicity of agrarian life did not necessarily require the law to be anything else. However, one overwhelming legacy of Rome had spread among the inhabitants of northern Britain – Christianity.

Canon law, regulation by an ecclesiastical authority, arrived with Christianity, making it necessary for various orders of clergy to read and write Latin for the documentation and interpretation of this law. As custodians of the knowledge preserved after the fall of Rome, clerics and monks were not tasked with writing something new, but rather with documenting answers and solutions found in scripture and what remained of the classical texts. It is from these Celtic monasteries, glowing embers of literacy and learning, that we find the earliest written laws native to Scotland.

At Iona, the centre of Celtic Christendom, the abbot Adomnán mac Rónán (624–704) produced a new kind of law. Having grown up in Donegal, Adomnán had witnessed the cost in innocent lives wrought by feuding and conflict among the Irish petty kings. Later in life, as he progressed through the monastical hierarchy, he discovered the authority his voice carried as successor to the great Columba. Gathering together Gaelic and Pictish notables, he and his monks instructed them to follow the *Cáin Adomnáin*, the Law of the Innocents. Though they may have regarded themselves as merely upholding the word of God, they had actually set out the first known systematic attempt to protect non-combatants from the brutality of war anywhere in the world: a kind of Geneva Convention of the Inner Hebrides. It included rules and corresponding punishments which, remarkably, were widely respected by the civil authorities, for a time at least. These rules were applied down to the individual, with one rule stating 'whoever slays a woman . . . his right hand and his left foot shall be cut off before death, and then he shall die'. Women were included as potential culprits as well, with the most serious crimes by women met with the sentence of being set adrift on a boat with a paddle and gruel, allowing God to decide their fate.

While the *Cain Adomnáin* contained much that was new, it also formalised many traditional Irish laws that the monks had been codifying over the previous century. As such, not only were these monks custodians of religious law, but they were also in a prime position as the only highly literate group in society to conduct the legal business of the newly Christianised rulers. Importantly, they would serve as the chief authorities in civil (Roman) and canon (Church) law, although disbursement of justice was mostly carried out by hereditary office holders. Nevertheless, despite the high aspirations of Adomnán, not all were equal before this law: the verdict often depended on social status and depth of purse. Scotland was not alone in this; there was not what we would consider a professional lawyer in the entirety of Western Europe at the end of the first millennium. Indeed, at this point, legal work was more function than role, with individuals loosely described as lawyers providing the functions of an advocate, a procurator or a notary but never describing themselves as one – it was only later that these roles became distinct. No historical legal practice can trace its origin this far back, but if they could chart the line of master and apprentice beyond what is written, some might find their deepest roots in these remote monasteries.

As northern Britain's bickering chiefdoms coalesced into what we might now recognise as Scotland, the beginnings of a secular legal profession began to emerge. The change into a more hierarchal, rule-based society was hastened by David I of Scotland (reigned 1124–53), who embarked on an ambitious programme of Europeanisation, which included the foundation of burghs, the arrival of continental monastic orders, and a division of the land between the old Gaelic nobility and families from France and the Low Countries. The accompanying pledges of rights and properties increased in complexity, so literate notaries became essential members of the community for recording business transactions, constitution of debts and the operation of feudal conveyancing, acting as a glue to the embryonic institutions of the early Scottish State. Nevertheless, these early notaries did not generally owe their position to the Crown: they derived their right to practise canon and civil law from either the Pope or the Holy Roman Emperor.

Copy of a charter by Robert the Bruce, c. 1323

The oldest document belonging to the firm is a notary's copy of a royal charter by Robert the Bruce. Dating from the end of his reign following the First War of Independence, it does not provide us with heroic tales of Bruce's exploits in his quest for a sovereign crown, but instead relates to the dowry of King Robert's sister, Matilda, to Hugh, Earl of Ross, following Matilda's death. As one of the king's favourites, Hugh continued to receive dowry payments after her death and was also awarded annual rents from the burgh of Cromarty.

This charter was clearly of significance among the elite of the kingdom, as it was witnessed by Bernard, Abbot of Arbroath and Chancellor of Scotland; Duncan, Earl of Fife; Patrick Dunbar, Earl of March; and Walter, Steward of Scotland. The first of these men, Bernard, is said to have drafted the Declaration of Arbroath – an inspiration for the American Declaration of Independence. The last, Walter, was the father of the first Stewart king, Robert II, with the new royal house named after their family's hereditary position of Steward.

How do we unearth lost names from this era? Letters, clients and stories were passed down through the generations, with some items belonging to the firm dating as far back as the early fourteenth century. Indeed, all that now remains of these early notaries are the documents that they created and held custody over. Among them we find a copy of a charter sealed by Robert the Bruce, land deeds of the expansionist Earls of Ross, and a charter of ferry rights at Queensferry sealed by James VI and Queen Anne. Notably, Anderson Strathern also holds a papal bull of Pope Clement VII addressed to Donald, Abbot of New Fearn (Ross-shire), confirming to his abbey liberties and immunities formerly granted by Pope Urban IV. This monastery, known as the 'Lamp of the North' due to its pre-eminent position as a centre of learning, was one of the oldest churches in Scotland and was probably afforded special treatment in an effort to stem the tide of Martin Luther's call for reformation. Despite this, all that can be visited today is a small church constructed on the grounds of the old, with the abbey having been brought to ruin not by a mob fuelled by religious fervour, but rather by the gentle and erosive passage of time.

Some of Scotland's early lawyers would have been intricately involved in the attainment of such privileges, possibly acting as emissaries to Rome to plead the case for the Earl of Ross and Abbot of New Fearn. One of the most influential legal interventions made in medieval Scotland was a result of one of these legal pilgrimages, with several early lawyers convincing Pope Boniface VII in 1299 to reject King Edward I's claim to overlordship of Scotland, resulting in the papal bull *Scimus, Fili* (We Know, my Son). This maintained a long tradition of Scots lawyers appealing directly to Rome, with arguably more Scots than English lawyers at the papal court for much of the Middle Ages, given that Scotland had been granted status as 'a special daughter of Rome' by Pope Clement III in 1192. However, the rejection of overlordship was not enough to quell

Edward's ambition, and a second delegation, led by the early lawyer Baldred Bisset, set out to convince the papal court of Scotland's independent origin and sovereignty.

To do so, Bisset delved not into legal ledgers but into the realms of myth. He claimed that the Scots, ever seeking to upstage the 'Trojan' English, descended directly from ancient Egyptians, and it was Egypt from which Scotia, the pharaoh's daughter, set out with the Stone of Destiny. This ancient symbol of Scotland, the same stone upon which kings of Scotland were crowned at Scone, further added legitimacy to Scottish nationhood through its biblical associations with Jacob's pillow (the Stone of Jacob). Myth was met with cold legal reality as the English delegation pointed to the Treaty of Falaise (1174), which made the king of Scots subordinate to the king of England, although it was renounced by the Scots just a few years later. In the end, some time after the decisive victory of the Scots over King Edward II at Bannockburn, the Pope came down on the side of Scotland, sending an ampulla of holy oils to anoint David II, son of Robert the Bruce, as sovereign king.

Lawyers would not find their skills redundant in this liberated kingdom. Just as the Crown had sought to wrest control from external powers, a similar battle with internal enemies is revealed in the firm's archives. One bundle of documents, pertaining to the MacDonald Lords of the Isles, details land transactions that took place as part of a campaign to dominate Scotland's Gaelic north. This brought the MacDonalds into direct conflict with the Stewart monarchs: not only were the MacDonalds becoming serious rivals in terms of strength, but they had also displaced the despotic Stewart holder of the Earldom of Ross. Sometimes through diplomacy, sometimes through force, throughout the Middle Ages, James I, II, III, IV and V would haphazardly rein in the clans, garnering the political power to establish national institutions akin to those in England and France. This shift in power is evidenced by the increase in the number of charters under the direct authorisation of the king, such as a feu charter of 1505 made under the seal of James IV found among the documents.

The assertion of the Crown's dominance over the law also saw a phasing out of the creation of notaries by foreign rulers. Indeed, as Scotland's southern neighbour increasingly asserted its own sovereignty, the remaining vestiges of subservience to the Holy Roman Empire, which by the fifteenth century was debatably neither holy, Roman nor an empire, could not stand. As such, in 1469 the Scottish Crown asserted its own authority over the law, as the Scots Parliament passed an act stating 'Notaris . . . sould be maid be the King and not be the Emperour.'

With the gradual consolidation of legal authority under the single figure of the monarch, the jumble of Roman, local and canon law that made up Scots law was increasingly in need of organisation; this led to the establishment of the College of Justice in 1532. From this small institution sprang the civil branch of the supreme courts of Scotland, the Court of Session, with the criminal branch, the High Court of the Justiciary, finding its origin in the medieval Justiciars instituted by David I. The College of Justice also brought about a further professional body of lawyers, the Faculty of Advocates, and gained association with the Society of Writers to His Majesty's Signet and later the Society of Solicitors in the Supreme Courts of Scotland.

It was not long until these organisations crystallised into institutions: astute record keepers who took note of the lives of their members in much more vivid detail than they ever had before. As Scotland's bureaucracy swelled, the Crown had to increasingly rely upon a growing cadre of notaries and lawyers for conducting the king's legal affairs, and some were entrusted with the use of his personal signet for confirming official documentation. In 1594 this elite group became a society, the Society of Writers to His Majesty's Signet, which marked out writers in terms of prestige and elevated rights (such as tax exemption in the City of Edinburgh).

While the College of Justice and Society of Writers to His Majesty's Signet were predominantly founded to improve the law itself, they also acted as a garment of respectability for the less than respectable lawyer. As in the rest of Europe, corruption and debauchery were rampant, as evidenced in dodgy dealings in the narrow closes of Scotland's towns and cities, or bribed incompetence beneath the vaulted vestibules of the courts. This was recognised as a serious problem within the legal establishment, with John Ross of Montgreenan, a senator of the new College of Justice, remarking that 'the name and estimatioun of ane advocate is becum vyle'.

While this may be hyperbole – Scottish lawyers were a respected class and well educated compared with their European counterparts – it is undeniable that some brushed shoulders with more than a few shady characters. We see an example in a copy of a letter found among the discoveries, penned in 1694 by a leading lawyer and opponent of the Union with England, James Anderson.

In it, we learn of a case Anderson had become entangled in, and subsequently profited from. Anderson writes how he is gifted by the joint sovereigns William and Mary part of the estates of 'Daniel Nicholson and Marion Maxwell found guiltie of notour and manifest adultery', with an associate doctor of medicine John Eliot being found 'guiltie of delivering poyson to the said Marion Maxwell to be applied to the body of Jean Lands'. It seems the intention was not to kill Jean Lands, but to frame her for an attempted murder of Daniel Nicholson so that he might claim her fortune. The scheme was evidently foiled, with 'the sentence of death pronounced thereupon by the Lords Council of Justiciary'. After an initial compensation of £100 to Jean Lands for the process of the case, the remainder of the estates of the three individuals was seized by the Crown.

Soon after, the vast bulk of the estates made its way into the pocket of James Anderson as a gift from William and Mary, although for what reason remains unclear.

The paper trail formed by this expanding legal state leads us from the shadowed obscurity of the distant past to fuller figures. While a firm is generally thought of as having its origins in an unbroken chain of partners, it seems that the founding partners in the three primary branches of Anderson Strathern – John Davidson, Thomas Cranstoun, John Lumsden – continued their master's practice in all but name. This is seen not only in the strong familial bonds present in cases, but also in the transfer of premises, clients and documents from master to apprentice going back deep into the seventeenth century. With John Lumsden being admitted as a Writer to the Signet (WS) in 1701, John Davidson in 1749 and Thomas Cranstoun in 1786, we might consider 1701 as the earliest date of modern establishment. Further still, as we shall investigate, the line of masters and apprentices linked by inheritance of clients, premises and documents, extends back to John Skene and Cuthbert Miller – both admitted WS in the sixteenth century – and earlier. Just because these early years do not conform neatly with our modern perceptions of the anatomy of a legal practice, we should not deem them unworthy of investigation or recognition.

Nevertheless, in this case, the task of unearthing the 'master–apprentice' lineage is simplified considerably. By chance, several lines converge on a single figure – Alexander Stevenson of Montgreenan, a native of seventeenth-century Ayrshire. The reason for this is that John Davidson, founder of Strathern & Blair, had the master George Balfour, and Thomas Cranstoun, founder of J&F Anderson, had the master Samuel Mitchelson. Both Balfour and Mitchelson were apprentices under Alexander Stevenson of Montgreenan. As the master of the founding partner of Bell & Scott was the apprentice of John Davidson, that historical practice converges here also.

Though little can be found relating to Stevenson's business upon his arrival in Edinburgh in the early 1700s from his home near Kilmarnock, a scrap of documentation suggests he helped process bills of sale for stock in the Company of Scotland – Scotland's disastrous attempt at establishing a colony in Panama. (One such receipt was held up until 1979, noting the then huge contribution of £200 by Sir Alexander Jardine.) Some thirty years later, Stevenson is listed as an elder of the Kirk, with his name also coming up as a director of 'The Orphan Hospital and Workhouse at Edinburgh'. While the Dickensian horror of the workhouse is in many cases true, when first established they were charitable endeavours to lift the population out of poverty. At any rate, it appears that Stevenson was a highly active member of society in and around Edinburgh at the cusp of the Enlightenment.

He may have been a visionary or a villain, or perhaps both. Without the discovery of a cache of personal letters and diaries, we will never really know. Stevenson and early figures like him, though more fleshed out than their predecessors, are nonetheless still preserved by paper alone. As well as being a joint father of the firms, Stevenson simplifies our exploration deeper into the past because we can follow a single chain of Writers to the Signet back from him, with each generation inheriting a position of eminence within legal society. It is through these antique chains, once forged by master and apprentice, now lawyer and trainee, that we can find the earliest predecessors of those few firms with pre-Enlightenment origins.

Before Stevenson, one name emerges in the firm's records time and time again: Sir John Skene, Lord Curriehill (1549–1617), a judge, ambassador and prosecutor who was appointed a notary during the reign of James VI. The king would be rewarded for his patronage as Skene went on to secure Princess Anne of Denmark as James's future queen. While James famously had a sexual and romantic preference for men, which he openly acknowledged at court, the marriage proved to be a loving one by the standards of the day, as well as politically advantageous. Skene, described as 'good, true and stout' by one contemporary, travelled widely across the northern countries of Europe, studying at the University of Wittenberg in 1570 and serving as ambassador to Holland from 1591. At least one of the three iron chests were likely cast in northern Germany in the late sixteenth century, so it is possible that Skene may have been the original owner.

As joint Lord Advocate to James VI from 1589 to 1594, Skene also had a more harrowing predilection. Having travelled to Denmark with James VI, the party experienced first-hand the large-scale witch hunts that were spreading throughout much of Europe at the end of the sixteenth century. The return voyage to Scotland was rough, and the royal ship, upon which James and his Lord Advocate were travelling, was nearly ship-wrecked. As the skies and seas turned violent, the royal party were forced to seek refuge in Norway for several weeks, and a terrified James became convinced that dark, occult forces conspired against him in a diabolical pact. He was not alone, as back in Denmark a tribunal was set up to find the demonic source of the storms, resulting in the burning at the stake of two women who claimed to have conjured the storm to disrupt the safe passage of Queen Anne. After the storms had passed, the king, queen and Lord Advocate continued to Scotland.

Disembarking from the battered vessel at North Berwick, James attended one of the previously rare witch trials given legal authority by the Witchcraft Act 1563. It would prove to be the first in a series of extensive hunts presided over by Skene, implicating more than 200 people over the course of two years. During Skene's tenure, several hundred individuals were tried for witchcraft, both men and women, with pricking, sleep deprivation and the crushing of feet used as a means of extracting confessions before the court. James VI himself supervised

Letter from the Court of Charles II to Ireland (1681) – document 2.1

Unearthed from the collection of antiquarian partner Alexander Duncan was a letter from Edward Conway, 1st Earl of Conway, which details intrigue at the Court of Charles II in 1681. The Irish noble writes to his brother of the rumours that the Duke of York, Charles's brother and the future James VII and II, was to return to court and be made heir, a huge controversy at the time given James's explicit Catholicism. Conway states 'There hath been great discourse in this Towne of the Duke of Yorkes returne to Court, but there is nothing of it.' Furthermore, Edward tells his brother that his wife has been 'sworne one of the Ladys of the Red Chamber to the Queen' and discusses how, should the French take Luxembourg, 'it will certainly necessitate his Majesty to call a Parliament'. Intrigue is layered upon intrigue.

Conway was the Secretary of State for the Northern Department, which was responsible for foreign affairs with Protestant states in northern Europe, and was seriously opposed to the designation of Charles II's brother, the Duke of York, as heir to the throne, a stance which may have cost Conway his position and reputation. Two years after this letter was written, Conway was dismissed in 1683 for 'crimes and misdemeanours . . . either in relation to the King's person or his public negotiations or transactions with foreign ambassadors, or in not rightly pursuing the King's instructions to ambassadors abroad'. After this fall from grace he retreated to the newly constructed Ragley Hall (Warwickshire) and died shortly after, aged about 60. The cause of his death is unclear.

many of these tortures, writing a book, *Daemonologie*, on his findings, and it is said that Skene's hunger for the hunt was just as ravenous.

Among professional lawyers there was a much lower rate of conviction (16%) compared to ad hoc local courts (90%), but they nonetheless gave the dignity of legal sanction to what would become one of the most extensive series of witch trials in all of Europe. Around 4,000 people were tried in Lowland Scotland for witchcraft, a much higher rate than England, with over 1,500 executed, often by a combination of strangulation and burning. The law's inquisitorial and decentralised attributes were among the primary motivators for such dramatic rates of persecution.

The paper trail of historical legal documents grows cold as law moves from profession to function. Pushing through the line of master and apprentice we arrive at the earliest verifiable lawyer in our history, Cuthbert Miller, a writer and notary born in the middle of the sixteenth century. It is most likely he began practising law, after apprenticeship, during the early reign of James VI, whom he may have encountered in the medieval roaming Parliament of Scotland, a body in which he held a seat. Little else can be known about him, unless another chance discovery is made. He is now as distant from us as we are from those in the twenty-sixth century, a silent partner in a very old tale.

2

The Scottish Enlightenment: John Davidson

'A great man of learning and intellect reflecting honour on the Scottish metropolis . . .'

Crumbling medieval high rises, narrow streets doubling as latrines, an empty palace and a redundant castle crammed onto the narrow slope of a dead volcano: this was Edinburgh's Royal Mile in the wake of the Union – a precarious thoroughfare hosting businesses and institutions great and small. With Crown and Parliament in faraway London, the over-proud institutions of university, Kirk and courts vied for the morsels of power that had survived the Treaty of Union in 1707. Living in this chaotic maelstrom were over 40,000 people, including David Hume, Adam Smith and our early historical partners. Change was in the pungent air: Edinburgh had begun its metamorphosis from 'Auld Reekie' into the 'Athens of the North'.

An altogether different transformation was occurring in the Clyde Valley. The city of Glasgow had held a significant position in Scotland since the Middle Ages, drawing influence first from its cathedral and later from its advantageous position on the Clyde. Nevertheless, Glasgow paled in significance to Edinburgh, and at times had struggled to be counted among the pre-eminent settlements of Scotland. With the opening of transatlantic trade following the Union with England, however, Glasgow became a boom town. So-called 'Tobacco

Lords' monopolised trade with the Americas, the Clyde was made suitable for ship building, and the coal beneath the surrounding countryside fuelled the factories along its banks. As in Edinburgh, poverty dwelt alongside wealth: the profits from slavery were spent on opulent, palatial residences in the Merchant City while peasants left their ancestral crofts for the slums of the growing Empire. Evidence of the slave trade remains in the city's street names – Virginia Street, Jamaica Street, Kingston Bridge – with Buchanan Street and Glassford Street named after those who profited from the slave trade.

The wealth generated was so great that in less than half a century Scotland went from among the least developed countries in Europe to at least the third most urbanised in the world. Yet it was beneath the cloisters of the city's university that Glasgow's longest-lasting contributions to the world were conceived. There, the foundations of modern philosophy, science and economics were laid by figures such as Francis Hutcheson, Joseph Black, Thomas Reid and James Watt. Under the aegis of these two cities the Scottish Enlightenment was born, but it is in the sleepy burgh of Haddington that our story begins.

John Davidson was born in Haddington in 1724. As the son of a bookseller, a respectable position but by no means an elite one, his early years were filled with ready access to knowledge and literature generally reserved for only the wealthiest in society, and certainly far removed from that available at Haddington's Kirk School. Religion and learning were then inseparable, and Davidson was given a considerable dose of both, not only in the classroom and the bookshop, but also by his father, who served for a time as a commissioner for spreading the reformation to the Highlands. These influences drove Davidson to a career in the law.

Having proved himself to have an excellent intellect, Davidson embarked on legal study at the University of Edinburgh. His course of study, spanning the middle part of the 1740s, overlapped with the Jacobite Rebellion, a conflict in which he played an active, albeit inglorious, part. As a lowland Presbyterian, Davidson joined the small student militia formed to oppose the usurper as he pressed down from the Highlands to take the Scottish capital. However, the city was ill prepared, with its dilapidated medieval walls and meagre garrison unfit for service. When the Bonnie Prince reached the walls of the city, the councillors threw open the gates in a bid to avoid a siege they could not win. Upon entering the city, the prince declared his father king of Scotland and himself regent, with the amassed Jacobite army set loose to paint the town red. Might Davidson have been swept up in the lavish celebrations in and around the Palace of Holyroodhouse, a Jacobite for one night only? It is impossible to know. But when the Jacobites eventually failed in their cause, the fragility of the Union, and the relationship between lowlanders and highlanders, were plainly exposed.

As the last vestiges of the Rebellion fizzled out, Davidson concluded his academic studies and was made an apprentice under an experienced lawyer – George Balfour – for the practical stage of his education in the law. As with generations before and after, Davidson would be tasked in this apprenticeship with abundant note taking, errand running and paperwork, but also given more significant work as a trusted partner in what was often a one- or two-person operation. Following the completion of this apprenticeship, Davidson was admitted as a Writer to the Signet in 1749.

What do we know of the personality of this ambitious, and newly independent, 25-year-old? From surviving letters, it is plain to see he was determined to make a name for himself; as the son of a bookseller he had to prove himself more than most of his peers. We also know, from various accounts, that he was well known for his crude sense of humour. This perception appears to have its origins in his

Letter Appointing a Dutch Quartermaster on the Day of the Battle of Prestonpans

This fragile and heavily damaged commission appoints an unknown Dutch soldier as a quartermaster on the day of the Battle of Prestonpans – one of the early Jacobite victories in the Jacobite rising of 1745. The commission is signed by the elderly John Dalrymple, 2nd Earl of Stair, safe in London, far away from the Highland Charge of the 2,500-strong Jacobite force. What remains of this tattered document is spattered with red droplets, leaving us to speculate what the fate of this new officer may have been.

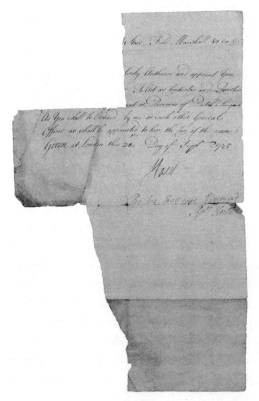

Commission for a Dutch Quartermaster at the Battle of Prestonpans signed by General Stair, 1745.

association with Henry Home, Lord Kames, an older, highly respected, yet outrageously outspoken, judge who was known for taking on promising protégés. As well as Davidson, Kames offered patronage to the up-and-coming James Boswell, Adam Smith and David Hume – friends of Davidson who formed a tight circle within Edinburgh society and would go on to lead the Scottish Enlightenment.

The Scottish Enlightenment falls into a category of historical turning points that cannot be described through a battle, an invention or a revolution, but rather through its creation of ideas which we now take for granted. In my view, it can be described through the attributes of Kames, characterised as he was by an irreverent humour, practicality and egalitarianism in contrast to the more exclusive and elusive intellectuals of continental Europe. It was in the pubs, not in the coffee houses, that the Scottish Enlightenment was born. For example, as Kames bid his sombre farewells to the other leading judges of Scotland on his retirement at age 87, he is reputed to have turned back to the grim room and exclaimed 'Fare ye a weel, ye bitches!' In fact, throughout his life he was well known for using this particular term, frequently referring to the prosecution and defence as 'bitches' in cases at the Court of Session, and right to the end he exclaimed to his doctor, who had asked why he was still dictating letters on his death bed, 'ye bitch . . . would you have me stay my tongue in my cheek till death comes to fetch me!?' Again, he epitomises another aspect of the Scottish Enlightenment – the prodigious output of its contributors.

Among Kames's contributions to the Enlightenment was the concept of the social evolution of society, a tradition continued by figures such as Adam Smith and Karl Marx, in which he proposed that social evolution was divided into four categories: hunter-gatherer, pastoral, agrarian and commercial. Scotland was his inspiration, as he, rather insultingly, saw the land divided into these four epochs, with a herding

Highlands, agrarian Lowlands and new commercial civilisation in Edinburgh and Glasgow. The Western Isles drew the short straw, with Kames identifying the lifestyle of those in communities such as St Kilda as sitting closest to the original state of humanity. Tucked away in a footnote of a Victorian law lecture, we find evidence that not only did Davidson provide 'invaluable assistance' for philosophical and legal works such as these, but he was also known for 'imitating even the uninviting manner of Lord Kames'.

With the help of his influential and foul-mouthed patron, and the associated circle of protégés, Davidson gained a firm foothold in legal society. Having inherited several clients from Balfour and independently gaining others, he found himself acting for key members of the nobility including the Earl of Findlater, the Duke of Hamilton, the Duke of Buccleuch and, from 1778, the Crown. This position presented unique challenges, especially as many of the clients lived in London and could only communicate by letter, with considerable delays due to the distances involved. However, it also presented unique opportunities for client and lawyer alike, as Davidson became a go-between for members of the nobility and leading Enlightenment thinkers across Scotland.

It was during Davidson's patronage by Kames that he met and married Helen Gibson. It is unclear where they lived during the first years of Davidson's practice, but by the late 1750s Davidson already had plans for the expansion of his business. Away from the dingy closes of the High Street that lawyers generally operated in, Davidson performed some complex legal acrobatics to acquire land at the top of the Royal Mile and construct a dwelling closer to the castle than any other building in the city. This plan, which he put into action in 1757, brought about a bitter feud with the artist Allan Ramsay, who owned land adjoining the patch Davidson was building on. The disagreement, as evidenced in a series of letters between the two, held at the NRS, related to a large patch of land which their mutual landlord, Francis Charteris, had promised to Ramsay for free use but ended up renting to Davidson while Ramsay travelled Europe. This provoked a furious reaction, with Ramsay concocting a tale that Davidson had tricked Charteris into believing that he would give the land to Ramsay. To this effect, Ramsay wrote to Davidson:

> I will not grant you any Servitude upon my own Ground, by Virtue of your letter above recited, so that if you are as deeply entrenched in Law as you imagine, the Ground you pretended to purchase for me will become you own, and you will carry it off with the additional glory of having outwitted my Doer and Mr Charteris, notwithstanding all his Endeavours to keep his Promise, and to do a kindness to his old Friend.

Despite his widespread acclaim and celebrity, Ramsay was rebuked by Davidson, leaving them no option but to bring the case first to the city council, and then to the Court of Session. Here, the matter was finally resolved in Davidson's favour. The judges concluded that Davidson could retain his new building and lands, with the exception of a strip of land leading to Ramsay's home and another piece between the western face of the building and the castle esplanade. While Ramsay was now granted jurisdiction over these areas, he was prohibited from constructing or planting on the land. In this case, the pen was mightier than the paint brush.

Having settled the land dispute, Davidson established his presence at the top of the Royal Mile with gusto, apprenticing several promising lawyers and subsequently taking on John Home and Hugh Warrender as his apprentices and eventual successors. As time went on, Davidson became known for growing exotic herbs in his garden, sending them to parishes

Castlehill (home of John Davidson
and Hugh Warrender)

Castlehill, a large building at the top of the Royal Mile, was commissioned by John Davidson as both a home and law practice in 1757. Before the construction of the elegant Georgian building, the area had been a location for the burning of witches, now commemorated with a 'Witches' Well'. From the time of its construction it would have served as a base for the single-partner practice until new offices were built at 12 Charlotte Street by John Home. Established before the conception of a New Town, this building would have been among the most desirable addresses in Scotland for both a home and business, standing as it did just a short walk from the law courts and the Kirk's General Assembly, as well as the Writers' Court and castle. It may have also been a desirable position in the then squalid Old Town as, being at the top of the volcanic crag, less waste would have flowed past this building.

A brief account of the house exists in 'Allan Ramsay's Rise and Reputation' (Brown), stating that it consisted of three floors, an attic floor and a sub-floor and included a coach house and garden. Overall, the building was successively occupied by Davidson and his apprentice Hugh Warrender, who inherited it, for over 60 years. Following the death of Hugh Warrender, it fell into the ownership of Sir George Warrender. Sir George, known as Gorge Provender because of his gargantuan appetite, was an MP for Haddington described by his contemporaries as 'a fat, garrulous and rather stupid man . . . pompous, quick-tempered and coarse'. He allowed the building to fall into ruin, resulting in its demolition around the middle of the nineteenth century to make way for a water tank for the Old Town. This structure remains today, and can be seen on the right-hand side when walking from the Royal Mile to the esplanade of Edinburgh Castle.

View of John Davidson's home and practice (middle left) taken
from Edinburgh Castle battery.

for medicinal use. In a letter, he complains of being unable
to send a rhubarb root to a nearby parish as his gardener was
on holiday. From this prominent location, Davidson would
encounter leading figures of the Scottish Enlightenment daily,
not only conversing with them, but influencing their works
and ideas by contributing his resources to their own research.
As alluded to already, throughout his career he was connected
with David Hume, William Robertson, James Hutton, Adam
Smith, James Boswell and Robert Burns, becoming an integral
conduit between enlightened thinkers and the nobility.

Beyond the other protégés of Kames, the young Davidson
is recorded as encountering John Witherspoon, a Presbyterian
minister born in Gifford, who went on to be a signatory of
the American Declaration of Independence. Witherspoon
migrated to the Thirteen Colonies on the Atlantic coast of

America in 1768 and became one of the Founding Fathers. But he and Davidson had known one another for over a decade before he left for America. Their first documented meeting was through the Society for the Propagation of Christian Knowledge (SPCK); they were both members and Davidson was joint treasurer. Davidson is registered as in attendance at one of Witherspoon's sermons at Edinburgh's High Kirk in 1754. The SPCK ran around 160 schools at this time and was known for being more progressive than the austere Kirk schools, which were spread throughout the country.

The paper trail of the relationship between Witherspoon and Davidson is scarce, though their early lives had remarkably similar trajectories: they were born a year apart near Haddington and both studied at the University of Edinburgh, so it seems likely they would have known one another long before that recorded meeting. Like Davidson, Witherspoon was a prodigious worker; while Principal of Princeton College he found time to attend over 10,000 committee meetings relating to the foundation of the United States. Witherspoon brought an essential, distinctly Scottish, slant to the American Revolution, importing ideas of reason, division of church and state, and limited governmental powers from across the Atlantic. Centuries later, Davidson and Witherspoon share the distinction of having their biographies listed in the Library of Congress.

After Witherspoon's migration to the colonies, Davidson maintained a robust friendship with another reverend at the very top of the Scottish Kirk, the historian and principal of the University of Edinburgh Reverend William Robertson. Robertson is remembered today for writing an early and thorough history of Scotland, from the reign of James V to the present, setting out in detail the famous story of Mary, Queen of Scots. In the preface to this significant work, Robertson thanked Davidson, stating, 'The facts and observations which relate to (Queen) Mary's letters, I owe to my friend John Davidson, one of the Clerks of the Signet, who hath examined the point with his usual acuteness and industry.' Davidson was also credited by Bishop Thomas Percy as procuring him historical manuscripts for his own works from across the continent, describing him as a 'good friend' and a 'great man of learning and intellect reflecting honour on the Scottish metropolis'.

Within his own profession, Davidson also kept some unlikely friends. Chief among these was his tavern companion the eccentric Lord Monboddo, a lawyer and judge who is occasionally credited as being among the first thinkers to claim that humans and apes are descended from a common ancestor, and who had a particular fascination with the potential for humans to develop tails. Though the mechanism to develop this new tail was not elaborated upon, Erasmus Darwin made mention of Monboddo in some of his notes on this exciting new line of thought which his grandson, Charles Darwin, would bring to maturity. Perhaps Monboddo's beliefs would have been taken more seriously if he were not already associated with other unorthodox views, such as the merits of nudism and the medicinal benefits of 30-minute naked 'air-baths' every morning.

In *The Life of Adam Smith* (Ross), we are told that Adam Smith, the father of modern economics, was also assisted by his 'friend John Davidson, clerk to the Signet' in reading documents written in calligraphic charter hand which neither Smith nor the judge Lord Hailes could decipher. The documents in question were ancient corn prices kept by the Court of Session, important in that they were a measure of the prosperity of the nation over time, as well as an indication of the strength of the currency. It is no surprise then that some of this research influenced Smith's *Wealth of Nations* – one of the most influential works in history – and the several dozen rare books Davidson tracked down for Smith and other clients over the decades may also have contributed useful research. Letters from Smith to Davidson also show that Smith was occasionally a conventional legal client, obtaining Davidson's help on matters of importance and on more trivial matters such as helping him get his pocket watch repaired.

Davidson's life as lawyer and socialite were one and the same. This is especially clear in a remarkable letter, held at the NRS, from Davidson to his client the Earl of Findlater. The letter appears to be a response to Findlater's request for advice on a tutor for his son, to which Davidson offers his views on the chief candidate – Robert Liston – and the virtues of other potential tutors. To begin with, Davidson recalls that in a recent conversation with William Robertson he discovered that Robert Liston was to depart for Parma to become a tutor. However, 'ye article of religion stopped all the scheme': despite the intervention of David Hume, Liston was ruled out for his Presbyterian background.

Having clarified Liston's recent history and subsequent availability, Davidson moves on to question whether he would be a good choice for Findlater given his young age, drawing a parallel between Liston and the young James VI. Instead, Davidson suggests a tutor more in the model of Louis XIV, the Sun King of France – that is, one with a long and accomplished track record. In search of this alternative, Davidson notes that, in his and Reverend Robertson's opinion, 'Dr Smith' is currently the greatest of Scots thinkers and as such should be considered. At the close of the letter, Davidson concludes that, although his friend Adam Smith would be a remarkable choice of tutor, Robert Liston would be more readily available. Findlater took Davidson's mixed advice and had his son educated by Liston. The son, who would become earl following his father's suicide, continued as a client of Davidson's until he fled to Europe in a self-imposed exile. This was partly due to his public homosexuality, which might have been overlooked had he not also made powerful enemies. Most notably, he was pursued through the courts for insulting the Duchess of Gordon, who had recently had a ship named after her: he was overheard remarking, 'I aye kent the Duchess had a brass neck and a brazen face, but I niver kent she had a copper arse.'

Davidson's role as a key link between Enlightenment figures and aristocratic clients is reasonably clear. The value of this connection was realised by Davidson in 1783 when he helped bring these two groups together as a founding member of the Royal Society of Edinburgh (RSE). As one of the first scientific organisations of its kind in the world, it required not only eminent thinkers but also patrons, and as a founding member of the society Davidson helped the Duke of Buccleuch – a friend and client of Davidson – to be elected as the RSE's first president. The RSE stood in contrast to its then well-established English counterpart, with the new RSE wading into some of the most controversial scientific, political and theological debates of the time. Davidson may have witnessed one such revolutionary moment: James Hutton presented his ground-breaking *Theory of the Earth* to the society in 1788. To little fanfare, Hutton made the first unified and extensive argument for an ancient and ever-changing Earth, or, as Hutton put it, a world with 'No vestige of a beginning, no prospect of an end'. This theory, flying in the face of millennia of religious doctrine, explained through empirical observations that the Earth was a product of natural laws and processes as opposed to divine interventions and biblical floods, helping to move the study of the Earth away from what some regarded as an eccentric hobby towards modern geology.

Having helped some of his compatriots revolutionise history, economics and science, Davidson tried his own hand at expanding human understanding. With his specialised knowledge of law and history, he focused on improving contemporary understanding of the origins of Scots law – a mix of civil and common law originating deep in the Middle Ages and unique to Scotland. Chief among these was his tract on the *Regiam Majestatem*, the earliest surviving digest of Scots law dating from the early fourteenth century. This had long been regarded as evidence of Scots law's distinctively independent origin, but brushing aside nationalistic pride Davidson, building on works by his predecessor John Skene, demonstrated that the *Regiam Majestatem* was largely based on the much older *Treatise on the Laws and Customs of the Kingdom of England* written by Ranulf de Glanvill. This provided a very early overlap between the law systems of Great Britain, though far from a total convergence: Scots law included the Celtic *Laws of the Brets and the Scots* and contemporary canon law.

Davidson also penned a tract on the Black Acts of 1584, laws passed under James VI which controversially tried to establish royal supremacy over the Kirk. Then, as now, leading figures of the day desired a historical understanding of the founda-tions of the identities of Scotland and England, and Davidson was keen to show that many ills blamed on the new kingdom of Great Britain, such as the dilution of Scotland's zealous reformation, had much deeper roots in the former kingdom of Scotland. These tracts were shared among the intelligentsia of the Kirk, the university and the legal establishment, and led to a better understanding of the formation of law in Scotland. To crown this achievement, the unpublished but widely circulated works were given engravings by Andrew Bell, the co-founder of the *Encyclopaedia Britannica*.

Despite forays into intellectual pursuits, Davidson's prodi-gious output was primarily focused on his heavy burdens as Crown Agent, prosecutor for the State and private lawyer. As the portrait engraver John Kay said, he operated 'for the greater part of his life . . . the most lucrative and respectable business in Edinburgh'. Kay provides us with the only representation of Davidson, a black and white illustration showing a smil-ing, bewigged and plump figure wearing a tricorn hat in conversation with Lord Henderland, George Paton, Lord Monboddo and James Hutton (see plate section). Between Monboddo and Hutton is a small monkey looking up at the pair, a nod to Monboddo's then-ridiculed theories on the origins of humanity.

Beyond Scotland, Davidson was also considered a significant patron for individuals seeking a career in the East India Company or in London. As Crown Agent in Scotland, and lawyer for landed clients who would sometimes pursue cases in the House of Lords, Davidson frequently had to visit London on business. There, he developed an important relationship with Drummond's Bank whereby he would help transfer the fortunes of merchants in the Far East and India back to Scotland, often in the form of diamonds and gold. The 45½-hour coach journey, laden with precious materials, along the Great North Road between London and Edinburgh would not have been for the faint hearted, especially in the age of highwaymen. But Davidson may have been fortified for the journey, for he never failed to take a large crate of whisky with him when he travelled south, much of which would be shared with his thirsty London clients. One commented, in reference to the 3rd Duke of Buccleuch, that 'I believe His Grace is afraid of you forgetting your Dram Box, but I say, no fear of that.'

Davidson was not short of business, with almost half of all administrators in India being of Scottish origin, and Scots making up a disproportionately large part of the overseas military, merchant and political establishments: Scots were the most proactive imperialists in the British Isles. Indeed, Davidson even contributed to this diaspora, as he was intimately involved in transporting, via Glasgow, 'felons to the colonies'. Along with many of his fellow Scots, high and low, he felt passionately in favour of the fledgling Empire, his enthusiasm stemming perhaps in part from those few days in the student militia defending the embattled Union. Fifty years

Adam Smith's Dispensation and Assignation to Robert Balfour Ramsay (1754) – document 2.3

Among the items rediscovered at Anderson Strathern is a remarkable 15-page legal text written by a notary on behalf of Adam Smith to settle a long dispute over land rights with the Balfour family, who were clients of the historical partner John Lumsden (d. 1757). The document begins by stating that 'Me, Adam Smith . . . Professor of Philosophy in the University of Glasgow . . .' had inherited the right to collect rents on a few pieces of land in Fife following the early death of his father. It then goes on to describe a protracted, decades-long legal battle with Margaret Balfour to claim them. Margaret Balfour was rather down on her luck at this time, not only having lost her brother to the Jacobite cause in the 1715 Rising but also having been recently embroiled with rebel sympathisers in the Rebellion of 1745. The case for the young Smith to claim his backlogged rents, which were calculated as being in the thousands of pounds, was taken to the Court of Session in Edinburgh, where Smith won the case. Following this, a wealthy relative of Margaret, Robert Balfour Ramsay, saved Margaret's skin by purchasing her land and debts, and with this document agreed not only to pay off debts owed to Smith, but also to purchase his rent-collecting rights. Smith, then at the beginning of his career as a public intellect, agreed to this with enthusiasm. As was the custom, Smith confirmed in the document that he would go about 'delivering to him or them . . . Earth and Stone of the ground of the said lands, a penny of money and other usual symbols' to represent his relinquishing of the land. Smith's signature is featured on every page, and there are correctional notes in his hand in the margins. As Adam Smith destroyed most of his own personal correspondence, few items such as this survive, and almost nothing is known of his early life. This early brush with the law and finance may have influenced his subsequent belief in investment and innovation to increase national productivity, and an opposition to land-owning elites exploiting their feudal dues.

after the Rebellion, as machinations in France again threatened the new British state, Davidson spoke of the 'unrivalled constitution' of Great Britain – regarded by some contemporaries as the 'perfect covenant' between a constrained crown and a property-owning elite. Davidson's proto-patriotism was also seen following the American War of Independence, when one of his clerks told an author who had written a book of naval tactics that Davidson 'yet entertains the hope that Great Britain shall command the ocean'.

As we have seen, the work of John Davidson primarily took place behind closed doors, but one case totally captivated the public imagination. The case in question gripped all of Europe, causing furious division of rich and poor alike, with Hume, Kant and even Voltaire wading in to the debate. It is little known today, but at the time it was inescapable. The Douglas Cause had it all: an heiress who ran away with an old soldier, twins abducted at birth, feuding among major celebrities, and incredibly high stakes – not only the title of Duke of Douglas but by some reckonings the largest personal fortune in the world.

It all started decades earlier when the 48-year-old Lady Jane Douglas moved to France soon after a secret marriage to Colonel John Stewart in 1746. As sister and heir to the childless (and suspected insane) Duke of Douglas, she was among the most eligible bachelorettes in Europe, albeit one deemed beyond child-bearing age. Even at this early stage, Davidson was involved – his client the Duke of Hamilton stood to inherit the Douglas dukedom and estate upon the death of Lady Jane should she remain childless.

But she didn't. After moving from place to place in France for two years under a false name, Lady Jane returned to Scotland with twin boys, threatening to bump Hamilton down the line of succession. When Lady Jane and one of the twins died in 1753, the old Duke of Douglas recognised the surviving twin,

Archibald, as heir. In 1761, the duke died and Archibald inherited the title and estates, but the Duke of Hamilton would not let go without a fight. He sent Andrew Stuart of Torrance, a confidante of Davidson, to uncover what really happened in France.

Following his arrival, Stuart set about retracing the couple's steps. Tracking down their former home in a small town outside Paris, he was told by locals that a devious yet aristocratic foreign couple had bought one baby from a glass maker and another from a 'rope dancer' before vanishing completely at the time of Lady Jane's elopement. If this foreign couple were in fact Lady Jane and John Stewart, besides the not insignificant issue of being the victim of child snatchers, Archibald would have no claim to the Douglas estate and Hamilton would inherit a second dukedom. The case was anything but clear, but with little to lose and everything to gain, Stuart's initial findings were brought before the Court of Session in 1762. Over the next five years more than 1,000 pages of statements were taken, 24 lawyers made speeches, and 15 judges presided over the case, racking up a total legal cost of more than £100,000. Perhaps the costliest legal case in history to that date: the huge transfer of money was surpassed only by the continent-wide bets placed on the outcome.

No one was spared from taking a side. Hume, Smith and Samuel Johnson – friends of Davidson – came down on the side of Hamilton; others, such as James Boswell and Voltaire, favoured Douglas. Eventually, with court and country split down the middle, Robert Dundas, the Lord President of the Court of Session, cast his deciding vote in favour of Hamilton.

Absolute chaos ensued. The Edinburgh mob, which had taken to the romantic story of eloped lovers, was furious and issued death threats to Dundas. Despite the victory for Hamilton, the case was far from over. Upon hearing the outcome, Douglas appealed the case to the House of Lords. With the amassed legal entourage travelling down to the highest court in the land, it met with a dramatic climax in London – but not in the law courts. Emotions were at boiling point. During deliberation in the Lords, Davidson's friend Andrew Stuart was accused of being a serial liar by one of the Douglas lawyers, leading to Stuart challenging the lawyer to a duel. A crowd amassed before the old Palace of Westminster to witness the stand off. The two drew pistols, took several paces and fired. Neither hit the other, both would live on to fight the case, but honour was restored. However, honour alone was not enough to win the day, as later the judges ruled unanimously in favour of Douglas, overturning the judgement of the Court of Session. Upon hearing the news, the Edinburgh mob erupted into celebration. They tore through the streets of the city, broke in to the Palace of Holyroodhouse and ransacked the Duke of Hamilton's apartments, with prominent supporters of Hamilton having to flee the city until the military intervened to restore public order.

Legal wrangling would continue for many years after, with Hamilton eventually winning a portion of the estate, but not the dukedom. Davidson unfortunately left remarkably little correspondence regarding this chapter in his life. But what does remain is a short, curious note dating from several years later, from Adam Smith to Davidson. In it, Smith remarks that they must 'never speak again' of certain secrets they uncovered during the thousands of hours of investigation into the Douglas Cause. With nothing more said on the matter they were evidently successful. Archives all over the country are stuffed with letters between Hamilton, the Duchess of Hamilton and Davidson. Further excavation may yield the secrets taken by Smith and Davidson to the grave.

Following this dramatic saga, despite the mixed result, Davidson attained a new level of personal influence, becoming the primary nexus of the legal establishment. He maintained this reputation until his death. This position found form from 1778 in his position as Deputy Keeper of the Signet, the de facto head of the Society of Writers to His Majesty's Signet. The society he inherited was struggling for relevancy. It had fallen far behind the Faculty of Advocates in what it could offer its members in terms of resources, and its medieval, cramped headquarters was proving an expensive burden for members.

When Davidson took up his position, his first act was to rationalise how members paid their admittance fee, thus raising the vital revenue required for modernisation and expansion. Davidson invested the proceeds in the development of the society's diminutive library, transforming it into a gargantuan collection. Under his leadership, the library increased in size to well over 3,000 items, 90% of which were not directly related to the law. The result was not only a practical resource for the members but also an intellectual tool for the profession to broaden expertise beyond formal confines. Shortly after Davidson's death, the society had to construct a new building to hold the vast number of books accumulated, as they could no longer be accommodated inside the Writers' Court headquarters. This led to the establishment of the modern-day Signet Library on Parliament Square, capable of holding nearly 200,000 volumes. Though Davidson's name is buried deep in historical annals today, the bookseller's son must be credited with injecting a considerable quantity of written knowledge into the veins of an Enlightenment dependent upon empirical evidence.

Despite professional acclaim, Davidson's later personal life was mired by tragedy. At some point in the 1790s the Davidsons lost their only son, an officer in the British Army, who died in combat while at war with revolutionary France, a conflict his father had feverishly lauded. Soon after that, Davidson's wife Helen also died, leaving just Davidson and Hugh Warrender at Castlehill. With no surviving children, Davidson planned to leave his Lothian estates to his cousin Joseph Davidson, on the condition that should Joseph fail to have any children the estates should be then divided between Henry Dundas and William Miller, a distant relation.

Davidson died while in office as Deputy Keeper in 1797 at Castlehill. He had initiated the creation of one of Britain's largest historical libraries, made substantive contributions to the Enlightenment, and left a number of literary works in his own right. By the time of his death he was among the foremost residents of the city, with the electoral roll listing him as one of only 96 men in Edinburgh eligible to vote. He was listed at the 15th position out of the 96, ranked by seniority, the most senior lawyer in enlightened Edinburgh. His clerk Hugh Warrender, who had lived with Davidson, would continue to practise law from the house at Castlehill, while Davidson's apprentice John Home would eventually establish an office in Charlotte Street, the home of part of the firm for the next two centuries.

Where previously ancient manuscripts were revered as the only legitimate sources of wisdom, figures such as Davidson presided over the rationalisation, accumulation and improvement of knowledge. It is fair to say that this crude, gregarious, literary lawyer helped bring Scotland, and the world, into the modern age.

3

Laws of Empire: Alexander Duncan

*'Before my mind was immersed in the drudgery of
public business, and the sordid thirst after gain, its
tone was not inelegant or uncultivated . . .'*

While the eighteenth century saw some in Scotland inhabiting a world of ideas and philosophical argument, the imperial enterprise and international trade which poured out of the Clyde, Forth and Tay was generating far more earthly fortunes. Lawyers whose predecessors had primarily been occupied by feudal disputes now found themselves navigating new and lucrative channels of business built on the very best and very worst aspects of the human spirit. Like John Davidson, who remitted vast fortunes from London to Edinburgh along the Great North Road, these lawyers managed the murky affairs of Scots abroad.

Alexander Duncan, who was admitted as a Writer to the Signet in 1765, shared with Davidson a love of antiquities and literary endeavours, and is similarly regarded as the founder of one of Anderson Strathern's historical predecessors, Bruce & Kerr. Unlike Davidson, Duncan was from a more typical background for a lawyer, being the son of the town clerk of Dundee and the grandson of its provost. Born in 1743, he was barely two when Bonnie Prince Charlie occupied Dundee, forcing Duncan's family to go into hiding for fear of reprisals over their government credentials. Following Jacobite control of Dundee, the Duncan family re-established their influence and Alexander went on to become one of fourteen distinguished Dundonian siblings. They would spread across the world – India, America, Europe, the Caribbean. One brother, Captain Henry Duncan, became flag-captain of HMS *Victory*.

Unlike many of his siblings, Alexander remained in Scotland to study law at the University of Edinburgh, and went on to be apprentice to his uncle-in-law James Graham, another historical predecessor of the modern firm. Graham was similarly not a native of Edinburgh, but was originally from Perth where his family had operated a small legal practice since the seventeenth century. In this business, Graham's father had described himself as 'Clericus Dunblanensis dioceses', a remnant of the episcopal era in the Church of Scotland's history. After leaving Perth, Graham set up shop in Glasgow, with a dispensation by the economist Adam Smith describing him as the 'Writer to the Signet for all Glasgow'. However, by the time Duncan apprenticed under Graham he was firmly based in the Scottish capital.

Duncan's apprenticeship was short-lived as his uncle-in-law died soon after bringing Duncan to the family firm, leaving his young nephew the sole proprietor of the business before having even been admitted a WS. In a profession in which it was so much more about who you knew than what you knew, Duncan found himself isolated – having to construct a career from what remained of his uncle's thin client base. Documentation held at the NRS suggests he largely sustained himself during this time through his work with the Balfours of Balbirnie although further investigation of several bundles of letters spanning 1763–67 would shed greater light on this period.

In 1768 Duncan married Mary Simson, the daughter of a Fife laird, and the couple started a family not long afterwards. As his proficiency in the law increased, he accrued the funds to purchase a home and office in Edinburgh's New Town – a mark of ambition, and a risk given that the project to extend

Edinburgh had only just begun. The building where he would practise law for the rest of his life – 2 Thistle Court – was one of the first buildings constructed on this grid and is the oldest building in the New Town today.

While the interior of that building is now a world away from when Duncan first moved in, we might still imagine what the eighteenth-century business would have looked like based on what Duncan left behind. As with other law practices of the time, the Duncans appear to have at first lived above the shop in a reasonably spacious apartment, with the lower floors dedicated to receiving guests and clients.

We also know the building housed an extensive personal library, an impressive status symbol at the time; this was revealed in a recently discovered catalogue of its contents written by Duncan. The library included items you might expect of a lawyer – legal tomes ranging from a near-medieval copy of the *Codex Justiniani* (a codification of Roman law) to notes on the Douglas Cause – but also religious tracts, comedies and what we might now describe as self-help books (e.g. *Instructions for a Virtuous and Happy Life*). The religious texts were not exclusively Christian: there was extensive coverage of Judaism and eastern religions, and a very early copy of the Qur'an in English. Duncan also held works on the slave trade, which were predominantly abolitionist in nature, along with works describing the nature, people, customs and cultures of the British Empire. In his line of business, this was essential reading.

This smoky, candle-lit house played host to historical oddities and letters piled high in tightly bound bundles. In fact, we can trace to Duncan the majority of items uncovered during the research for this book, including Adam Smith's dispensation and assignation, letters from the Court of Charles II, a wax privy seal of George III, a blood-stained commission from the Battle of Prestonpans and much more.

With each passing generation of lawyer this unique inheritance was divided and dwindled; we should be thankful that any part of the collection survived at all. Nevertheless, in search of blood, sex, fortune and murder, we need look no further than the collector himself. Interspersed among medieval writs and famous names, Duncan's own brush with scandal and tragedy can be carefully reconstructed.

In 1786 George Simson, Duncan's brother-in-law, embarked on a journey to India to work as a clerk for the East India Company (EIC) in the Bombay Presidency. At that time Bombay was a city divided, with British officials living on a well-fortified peninsula and Muslim, Hindu and Zoroastrian inhabitants living elsewhere in the city, trading with Europeans and each other. As a meeting place of East and West it was unlike almost any other city in the world, with fortune hunters from India, China, Portugal, Britain and Africa intermingling in the busy docks, marketplaces and inns. Having grown up with his elder sister Mary in the East Neuk of Fife, the teenage Simson would have found India an invigorating, possibly alarming, shock to the system.

As he stepped off a frigate fresh from half a year at sea, instead of a thriving hub of commerce he found a city in panic. Rumours were circulating that the European powers of France, Britain and the Dutch Republic were on the cusp of war. As Bombay had the only dry-dock in India capable of repairing and constructing modern warships, it was key to British naval supremacy in the Indian Ocean. And with a two and a half month delay in news from Britain, war fleets could appear on the horizon without warning. Within India, despite its strategic importance, the Bombay Presidency controlled only the hinterlands of the city and a few coastal ports, making it vulnerable to attack from Indian princes such as the ruler of Mysore, Tipu Sultan.

Journal of Messrs Francis and MacKrabie (1774) – document 2.5

Among Duncan's letters is a sixteen-page account of a journey from London to Calcutta in 1774. The diary was written by Sir Philip Francis, a politician who had been appointed to the newly established Supreme Council of Bengal, and his brother-in-law Alexander MacKrabie, who travelled as Francis's private secretary on the voyage. As the Suez Canal had not yet been constructed, the journey from England to India took more than six months. Francis, MacKrabie and roughly 170 others travelled from the docks at Dover to Madeira, the Canaries and down to Cape Town, over to islands off the east coast of Africa and finally to India.

The diary is full of observations on race, culture, religion and colonialism. As the writer passed Madeira, known then for its wine, he called it 'the seat of the elysium of the ancients', a nod to Plato's legendary island of Atlantis. At Cape Town he recounted more worldly spectacles, noting 'with respect to Dutch police, I can assure you that a man may be as effectively impaled at the Cape of Good Hope, as in Constantinople'. Travelling on to the Island of Joanna, off the coast of Tanzania, he discussed the reception they received from the local inhabitants: 'We dined with one of the principal men of the place who called us his brethren, and treated us in a family way, that is, he gave us a very bad dinner and expected to be paid for it.' In a slightly more surprising criticism, the writer observed 'they profess to be Mahametans [Muslims], but considering how scrupulous they are about ceremonies and how negligent of duties, one might easily mistake them for Christians.'

Upon reaching India the ship made frequent stops along the Coromandel coast to visit Indian rulers who sought to gain favour with, and make their authority known to, the new councillors. On a visit to the Nawab of Arcot's palace, the writer lamented East India Company regulations regarding bribery to favour a certain ruler, stating 'He [the Nawab] might, if the law had not put our virtue out of the reach of temptation, have presented each of us with a pearl, a

Diamond, or a Persian horse – such sweet remembrancers make lasting impressions.' The company intended not only to do business with these rulers but to bring them under their sphere of influence, as the writer makes clear when describing a banyan tree: 'It has been described a thousand times, yet I cannot help informing you that its branches descend till they touch the ground, where they take root and springing upwards become a new tree, that supports its parent. The progress of this wonderful tree is a perfect emblem of the true Principles of Colonisation.' Soon after this visit, the journal abruptly ends upon their arrival in Calcutta. There was work to do.

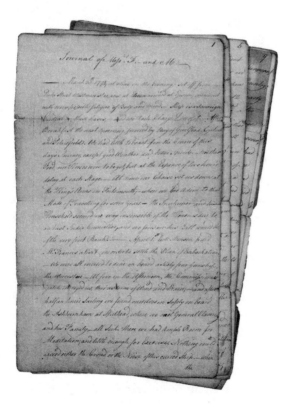

The front of the battered journal of Messrs Francis and MacKrabie, which details the journey from London to Calcutta, c. 1774.

Simson would have found himself far from being the only Scot in Bombay: the registers of EIC merchants show that at times nearly half of the merchants were of Scottish origin. His sister Mary had arranged for him to meet with two of them: Craufurd Bruce, the fifth son of a Lothian laird, and James Beck, a cousin of Alexander Duncan. Both merchants were also clients of Duncan, who handled their personal affairs in Scotland while they sought to amass a fortune abroad. James Beck had also been an apprentice of James Graham alongside Duncan, though his time with Graham did not end so amicably. In Beck's large collection of letters and legal transactions, which eventually landed on Duncan's desk, we are given a personal insight into the tumultuous lives of these families.

The raw tension of Bombay at the time of Simson's arrival is palatable. In one letter Craufurd Bruce writes to Beck 'I see nothing but evident ruin' as Bombay was 'totally unprepared' for a coalition between the French and Mysoreans. This fear was not irrational: in a recent war between France and Mysore the vulnerable city was briefly attacked causing widespread destruction and, to the horror of the merchants, substantial loss of revenue. The East India Company, a trading company that became a global empire more by accident than by design, had already narrowly avoided financial collapse in 1772 and 1783 as a result of such convulsions. At home, Britain had just lost the war with the Thirteen American Colonies and was disillusioned, for a short while at least, with its imperial project. Perilous conditions in India, coupled with natural problems of disease and dangerous travel, led to a mortality rate of 57% among British administrators in India. With the merchants clamped between two revolutions, the American and the French, life and profit teetered on a knife edge.

Following the rendezvous with his patrons Bruce and Beck, Simson was sent on to his lodgings at the residence of the governor of Bombay, Rawson Boddam. New letters reveal that Boddam was on the brink of a mental breakdown, as the company's private army demanded 'that the revenues [of the Presidency] should be exclusively reserved for the military'. These tensions, coupled with an official crackdown on corruption, including that of the governor himself, led to Boddam's superiors in Calcutta and London demanding his immediate replacement with a military governor shortly after Simson's arrival. Until that governor arrived, Andrew Ramsay, another Scot, whom Simson would live with, was to serve as interim governor, although he proved similarly vulnerable to the pressures of the job. Indeed, in one letter Bruce noted that 'Mr Ramsay is not very well right now' and stated that if Ramsay were to take up a post in Surat 'from the situation of his Nerves I think he could not stand it'. The second-in-command, Andrew Griffiths, was also noted as being 'very much depressed', with Bruce commenting 'I should regret much if he dropped.'

James Beck and Craufurd Bruce had also suffered a tumultuous few years since setting up shop in India, made additionally complex by their romantic entanglements before their departures from Britain. These entanglements are preserved in great detail in a bundle of love letters and erotic stories penned by James Beck, which eventually fell into Alexander Duncan's hands.

In one, we find something resembling an autobiography of the former apprentice. In it, James Beck states that he was born near Perth in 1748 into a landed, yet impoverished family. While he was still young, his father and siblings died in quick succession, and by the time he was 15 his mother had also passed away, leaving him an orphan in possession of a small estate which he lacked the means to maintain. Beck therefore left home to train under his uncle James Graham, concurrently with Duncan. It is likely that he also studied for a time at the university. This did not last, however, and soon Beck left Scotland at the age of 18, to work as a junior officer aboard a ship operating under charter to the East India Company.

When he returned to Britain, he discovered that his uncle
had died leaving him with a measly inheritance and 'not a friend
in the world'. He begged for patronage around the courts of
the south of England, targeting wealthy artists in Richmond,
Windsor and Hampton – squandering the very last of his
inheritance in the process. This itinerant phase notably brought
him to the home of the Tickells, a family of poets for whom he
would later pen his erotic tales. He probably subsisted like this
for five years, finding fitting employment only after an encounter with a director of the East India Company, John Manship.
The two grew close, leading to Manship offering the young
man a position as an EIC writer in Bombay. Accompanying
Beck were his servant and mistress Ann Caroline Bartlett, with
whom he would have five children in India and China. Beck's
will of 1777, made before he set off to a military campaign
north of Bombay, also implies he had at least one child with an
Indian woman.

While not raised in the same circumstances as Beck,
Craufurd Bruce was unable to depend on his father's estates
for a living, being the fifth son of a laird. However, his father's
connections managed to secure him a writership similar to
Beck – leading both to India.

In their fifteen years in India before the arrival of Simson,
the merchants Bruce, Beck and Stewart were prodigious in generating both fortune and offspring. It was common for these
merchants to have children with local women, and between
them they fathered at least seven children with women in India
and China. In the case of Bruce, apart from some brief mentions in an early will, it is difficult to trace what became of his
illegitimate children or their likely Indian mothers. What we
do know is that, on a return visit to Britain, Bruce met Jane
Smith, the daughter of a Lancastrian industrialist, with whom
he eloped to Gretna for a clandestine marriage in 1785.

2 Thistle Court (office of Alexander Duncan)

At the heart of the ordered grandeur of the Edinburgh New Town is an embarrassing anomaly. Tucked away between the wide thoroughfare of George Street and elegant townhouses of Queen Street, the former office of Alexander Duncan, 2 Thistle Court, was the Georgian New Town's false start.

The story goes that, before Duncan transferred his practice from the Old Town, the site was developed by notable resident James Young, who was offered £20 by Edinburgh City Council to construct the New Town's first building. However, instead of conforming to the 1767 grid plan set out by architect James Craig, Young decided to build four terraced houses off street with the intention of preserving a view of the Firth of Forth (now long gone). The dwellings were also constructed in rubble rather than the more expensive materials intended for the area.

It is uncertain when Duncan moved his practice to this address, but he was firmly in residence by the early 1780s as he was practising from this address at the time of the events involving the Bruces and Becks in India. But all was not well. In one letter from Duncan to Bruce at this time, Duncan recounts how he had spent nearly a year housebound, unable to work due to a combination of rheumatism and grief over the loss of his only son. Duncan's fortunes would improve as he continued to work from Thistle Court for a further 35 years.

Duncan's successors remained at Thistle Court for several years until expanding to larger, more modern, premises in Frederick Street and later Hill Street in the mid nineteenth century. Thistle Court still stands today, probably the oldest remaining building in the New Town and certainly among the most intimate.

On the return voyage to India, the newly married couple were accompanied by Bruce's sister, Jamima, a prospective bride for James Beck. This was to be a marriage of convenience:

convenient for Beck in that it connected his business interests with that of Bruce, and convenient for Jamima in that she had the security of a marriage to an affluent, successful merchant without the expectation of providing children. This was probably because Jamima's true name was James Thomas Bruce. We do not know, and may never know, why her parents moved from identifying her as their son to their daughter in childhood, but it is most likely that she was born intersex. As such, she would have been unable to conceive, and in a world where a wife's primary function was the continuity of her husband's line, this almost certainly prevented most matches.

However, when Jamima arrived in India, Beck was nowhere to be seen. He had been dispatched to Surat by the governor on secret business. Inconvenient though this may have been for the prospective couple at the time, it meant that their first interactions, in the form of letters, can still be read today. From the outset of this correspondence, it is clear Jamima's intersexuality had not stopped her enjoying an active sex life, as she explains in surprisingly frank terms that she had reluctantly left a lover in Scotland, known only by the initials 'M.G.', to be with James Beck. She also said she felt unable to promise any genuine affection for the lawyer and merchant. Indeed, as James pledges her his every attention and devotion, and describes the life they might have together, she laments that 'passion does not cease at the command of reason'.

In contrast James's letters are almost dripping with the sickly sweet sensibility of the era, especially as he acknowledges in an introspective moment that 'before my mind was immersed in the drudgery of public business, and the sordid thirst after gain, its tone was not inelegant or uncultivated'. Jamima is championed as the remedy he requires for his 'delicacy of feeling' to be restored. Nevertheless, as the match increasingly seemed doomed to fail, James decided to send a series of sexually explicit stories to Jamima which included among other things tales of women being forced into prostitution on the streets of London by their husbands, and a detailed description of the passionate 'embrace' of two young lovers, leading to pregnancy and abandonment. Talk about a red flag. James clearly had a unique way with women (and, we might deduce, men too).

Against all odds, the couple appear to have bonded over these stories, and Jamima finally started to come round to the match. This was also spurred on by their mutual difficulties with health – James struggling with his 'nerves' in a similar manner to many other company officials, Jamima's health deteriorating from an unknown illness under treatment with 'courses of mercury'. When James Beck returned from Surat, their courtship gathered pace albeit under the shadow of Jamima's deteriorating health. Their union also hastened the separation of James and his mistress Ann Caroline: Jamima sent her and the eldest children back to Britain.

In these years the prospects for the Bruces and Becks appeared rosy, but all was not well. Their business partner, Charles Stewart, another client of Alexander Duncan, was a chilling reminder of the mortal risks of their profession: he had recently been fed to a tiger.

Charles Stewart had been anticipating the thrill of battle from a safe distance following his commission in 1782 as the paymaster for the Bombay army in a new war against Tipu Sultan. It was a profitable position which would probably take him away from his affairs in Bombay for less than a year. These affairs included providing for his happy, and unorthodox, family, which comprised his Indian servant Champy and their mixed-race infants Patrick and Charlotte. His was still a very young family: on the eve of Stewart's departure for war, his son was around two years old and his daughter had been born just a few months prior. After his farewells, he joined the force led by General Mathews down the coast from Bombay,

Short Stories from Mr Beck to Mrs Tickell (c. 1770) – document 2.4

Included among Duncan's items are several short stories sent from James Beck of the EIC to Mrs Tickell, the mother of the Irish playwright Richard Tickell (as well as later letters to his future wife Jamima Bruce). Beck was 27 when he wrote the letters to Mrs Tickell en route to his life as a merchant in Bombay, and states their purpose as being to pass time in the 'barren deserts of Arabia'. However, though he presents the stories as fictional, several intimate references, errors and an explicit reference to their 'exact similitude to Truth' betray the autobiographical nature of the stories.

The stories themselves violently veer between the philosophical, the sexual and the domestic. For example, one consists of a letter from Horatio to Lysander recounting a story of a young Scot from a legal background pursuing an elegant debutante in Oxford. Later he comes into competition with another potential suitor who, using salacious techniques, forces the young man into poverty. Finally, following the ascension to a position of political power, the young man manages to turn the tables, and gains his lover's hand in marriage.

In another story, we are met with a young man of modest means, first embroiled in a love triangle, eventually having to flee in disgrace to the Caribbean due to his failure in wooing a wealthy heiress. Soon his former lover is on the cusp of being forced into prostitution by her abusive husband, who before carrying out the plans on his pregnant wife is murdered in a pub brawl. Beck also wrote a few more sexually explicit stories, unusually from the perspective of women. In these he managed to mention the word 'bosom' sixteen times in total, around once per page.

The most compelling aspect of these stories is the intended audience. For the 27-year-old Beck to casually trade erotic stories with an older upper-middle-class woman and her social circle shows a free expression that would surely cause shock in subsequent generations. His later letters were written for a much younger upper-class woman whom he had never met and intended to marry; however, they seem to have worked as he and Jamima were married just months after this exchange.

from which point they pushed into the Indian interior. There, they fortified the settlement of Bednore and dug in against a much larger Mysorean force, awaiting reinforcements led by Norman MacLeod of MacLeod. Stewart was there solely for administrative purposes, ensuring that the soldiers were paid, or at least promised pay in good time. He had not bargained on being subjected to a punishing siege, especially one they were about to lose. The reinforcements failed to arrive, and soon the entire army surrendered – paymaster and all – and handed themselves over to the mercy of Tipu Sultan.

The prisoners were treated with as much humanity as the Mysoreans had come to expect from the British. Following their capitulation, they were relieved of any valuables they might have, chained together and marched over 150 miles to the Mysorean capital. During this march, when one died in the line, the others had to drag the shackled corpse through the searing heat until they stopped for the night. The officers and Stewart were treated with a greater degree of comfort and were transported in a separate convoy at great haste for an audience with the Mysorean ruler. This would be no courtesy call. Tipu Sultan's reputation for sadistic punishment, and well-founded hatred of the East India Company, were common knowledge.

Accounts from Captain Henry Oakes and latterly James Forbes, a friend of the Bombay merchants, shed light on what happened when they arrived at the palace. In the Oakes account, it is claimed that Tipu Sultan met the senior military officers and 'Mr. Charles Stewart, the Pay-master' in his durbar. The prisoners were treated like honoured guests, waited on hand and foot by slaves amid the lush trappings of an Indian court. This was a disarming illusion. Forbes's account adds a little extra detail on what followed. It states that after being seated on the carpet 'they were each presented with a cup of poisoned coffee' which General Mathews at first hesitated in drinking. Then 'Mr Stewart, better acquainted with the sultaun's character, advised him to acquiesce, otherwise insult would be added to cruelty, and taking the cup intended for himself, drank it off. As the sultan had a penchant for feeding captured Europeans to his prized menagerie of tigers, we might assume that Stewart's resolve was to avoid such a painful end. If they were to be fed to the tigers dead or alive, the former would be preferable.

Before his fateful departure, Stewart left behind his own poisoned chalice. Expecting to return but understanding that the post did not come without risks, he hastily jotted down a one-page will in which, at first glance, he appears to leave his entire estate to his illegitimate, mixed-race children under the stewardship of Champy. The authorities did not quite see it this way: by the time the will was settled, his son had died and neither the mother Champy nor the remaining child, Charlotte, were considered eligible for the fortune. The issue largely lay with the caveat 'in case the said mother should prove again with child it is my Pleasure that the whole of my Estate be equally divided between the mother and the Children'. This was most likely intended to provide for the possibility that Champy should have another child in Charles's absence; however, by the time the will was settled the obvious heir was dead and, given that Champy had not 'proved' again with child, the estate was not divided, and she was left 'totally unprovided for'. Therefore, the estate was temporarily seized under the royal prerogative and placed in the administration of Alexander Duncan.

The mother and child, now destitute and homeless, were taken in by James and Jamima Beck. In hope that Alexander Duncan would be able to prove her daughter's right to the fortune, Champy accepted a painful offer. Her daughter Charlotte would travel to Britain with James and Jamima to press her claim to her father's fortune at the court of George III, after which she would be left with her father's family in Scotland. Champy would remain in India. The reason for this is not made explicit, but we might deduce her race, religion and class were the motivating factors, not to mention the great expense and risk of a transoceanic voyage. Understanding the opportunity this provided for her daughter, Champy accepted their separation.

In a way, this illustrates the complex attitudes to race that Beck, Duncan and others held at the time. Beck was prepared to make a perilous crossing to secure the inheritance of a toddler of mixed race. He also counted among his closest companions 'black merchants' in the city's markets, all the while owning several slaves; in early wills he even left these slaves, as property, to his business partner Craufurd Bruce. Similarly, while Alexander Duncan was willing to petition the Crown for the inheritance of Charlotte and held abolitionist sympathies, he nevertheless represented several Scottish slave owners with vigour. Both Beck and Duncan also sought to educate themselves in Indian culture and Arabic writing – which was more than could be said for most of the British in India – but almost certainly held the almost-universal western view of the cultural superiority of Europeans.

With Duncan, Champy and the Becks agreed to this course of action, James Beck, Jamima and Charlotte all set off for Britain. On board were 171 individuals, of whom 110 were seamen, 25 invalids, 24 passengers and 12 servants, all crammed into the tight confines of an East Indiaman ship, the *Rockingham*. Among the passengers were an EIC judge, a reverend, several merchants (including the Becks) as well as 'black servants' including Tom and Mary, who travelled with the Becks. The ship left Bombay under the command of Captain John Atkinson Blanshard on 22 February 1787; it would be the last sea voyage any of them would make.

As the voyage got under way, both Craufurd and Jane Bruce wrote to those aboard the *Rockingham* with increasing concern. In one letter to Jamima, Jane writes that she too had been ill and treated with bark and mercury, and her baby son, who could 'kick and fling as well as any Highlander', had been successfully inoculated against smallpox without any scarring. Jane also passed on details of high society that Jamima may have missed. This included the detail that 'Old Jenny Shank at last acknowledges herself to be old, she has entirely given up dancing and seldom goes out anywhere.'

To find out what happened aboard the ship as it crossed the Indian Ocean, we must now rely upon the entries in the preserved captain's log and what is known of similar journeys. Certainly, this would have been no pleasure cruise with 171 individuals crammed into tight confines for months on end, resulting in squalid, disease-stricken conditions for even the most elite of passengers. The captain's quarters were one of the few places of peace aboard such a ship. It was in this oasis of quiet, separated from the passengers and crew by timbers, that Captain Blanshard reported that their number had fallen by one. Just one month into the journey, he wrote in his log that 'at 2pm departed this life Mrs Jamima Beck and at 7 committed her body to the deep with the usual respectful ceremony'. Weakened by continual courses of poisonous mercury, the harsh conditions at sea and her unknown illness, Jamima Beck had died at the age of 28.

The loss of his wife deeply affected James Beck: although his relationship with Jamima had been brief and unconventional it clearly represented a positive stage in his life during which he could stave off his tormenting melancholy. The tragedy is made all the more troubling as the Bruces in Bombay, unaware of the death of Jamima for nearly a year, continued to write to her long after her death. The remainder of the crossing was hellish, with shipwreck narrowly avoided off the coast of Africa and a multitude of desertions, possibly including the servants Tom and Mary, at the remote Atlantic island of St Helena. Unusual in its detail and regret, the log also records that 100 gallons of rum were lost in a leak.

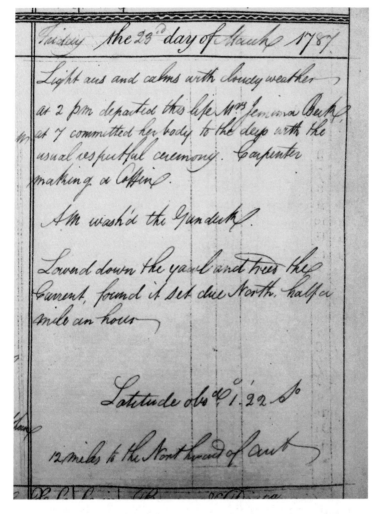

The captain's log entry from HMS *Rockingham* indicating the death and burial of Jamima Beck at sea, during her voyage from Bombay to Dover with her husband James Beck and Charlotte Stewart (1787).

Alexander Duncan was waiting for James and Charlotte at Southampton docks when they finally arrived half a year after their departure. Learning only then of the death of Jamima,

Duncan conveyed the two with haste to the court of the king at St James's Palace, where he put in motion the process of Charlotte's legitimisation. From there, Duncan took charge of the young Charlotte and transported her to Scotland.

Remaining in England, Beck, now lacking a wife, reunited with his mistress Ann Caroline and the children she had brought back to England with her, though this apparently gave him little solace. After spending time with them in Bath, he travelled to London and lodged a new and thoroughly detailed will. Shortly afterwards, Beck visited John Manship, his patron all those years ago and now second-in-command of the East India Company. Beck entered the residence on Sloane Street, where Manship and his elderly mother lived, but he was not to leave it alive. The morning following Beck's arrival, Manship informed the world of James Beck's suicide – a deadly shock which confounded both Ann Caroline and Craufurd, who could not understand why Beck would take so drastic a step. Given the uncertain circumstances around Manship's initial offer of patronage, we might speculate that James Beck's death was not by his own hand.

Upon receiving this news, Duncan immediately set off for London to put Beck's affairs in order. In doing so, he collected bundles of letters that Beck had left behind, representing a personal history until now entirely forgotten, but one deemed worthy of preservation by successive generations of solicitors. Duncan went on to liquidate Beck's now considerable estate, amounting to £36,000 in 1788, and divided it between Ann Caroline and their five children. They all lived in luxury for the remainder of their lives.

Despite being born into this morbid and precarious situation, the rest of Charlotte's life was happier. Assisted by Duncan, she was granted a full legitimisation under the Privy Seal of Scotland, which decreed her 'to all intents and purposes as if she had been procreate and born in lawful marriage and wedlock'. Cases such as this were the exception rather than the rule, as generally the instincts of the East India Company would entrap any potential revenue that might escape its structures. Indeed, the corruption, unaccountability and inhumanity of these sovereign merchants was so rampant that the traditionally laissez-faire London government had to directly intervene with increasing regularity, until, following the Indian Rebellion, the EIC was finally disbanded. Thankfully, Charlotte had escaped its venomous grip, and with Duncan's help was reunited with her father's family in Scotland. Years later, she went on to marry a Fifer who later became a champion golfer, with whom she had several children. She lived the rest of her life in St Andrews within sight of the sea, though never again crossed it.

As time passed, the Bruce family experienced huge financial success. Craufurd Bruce became an MP, and his son found international fame by helping the Comte de Lavalette to break out of a French restoration prison, and then eloping to the Middle East with Lady Hester Stanhope, a lover of Byron. Bruce would also help his nephew, Thomas Brisbane, to gain the position of Governor of New South Wales, leading eventually to that city being named in his honour.

George Simson returned to Britain soon after these events unfolded and joined Bruce in Parliament as an abolitionist MP. Their ill-gotten gains did not last, and eventually both found themselves bankrupt, with George Simson forced into a life of obscurity on what remained of his estate in Fife and Bruce's wife dying in genuine poverty. The pressure of the cocktail of tropical diseases, financial ruin and constant threat of war was a deadly one, and even when individuals had apparently succeeded, it is telling that Bruce, Beck, Stewart and Simson all met either an untimely death or financial ruin. However, our sympathy can only extend so far as they chose to pursue this all-or-nothing line of work, unlike many of their family, servants and slaves.

It seems that Duncan had certainly had his fill of imperial misadventure. Shortly after this period, exacerbated by rheumatism and the death of his son, he suffered something close to a mental breakdown, leaving his wife and two daughters to more or less run the business themselves – just one instance of the hidden role of women in eighteenth-century law. After a year of recuperation, Duncan managed to regain his ability to work, and went on to grow his practice to a greater size, including taking up work as a Crown Agent, allowing him to purchase the estate of Restalrig on the outskirts of Edinburgh. He continued to engage with the surviving subjects of the letters, and was involved with several other Scots imperial families such as the Johnstones of Westerhall.

Duncan managed to pass down the business to his nephew William Stephenson and another partner John Yule, though he would only relinquish his senior position with his death in 1821. He was among the last to be buried in a private tomb at the Old Calton burial ground, under the shadow of the mausoleum of Hume. To the end, Duncan continued collecting items of historical significance, a challenging task at a time when the past was so shrouded in darkness. Like the objects he collected, Duncan became a venerated relic, caught between the conflicting yet troublingly symbiotic forces of Enlightenment and Empire.

4

The Tangled Webs of Sir Walter Scott:
John Gibson

*'He has no more right than Burke and Hare had to
daft Tam's body . . .'*

As the era of the Enlightenment slipped away, Scotland was a
nation bursting at the seams with self-congratulation. It rapidly
mythologised itself as the world's intellectual capital and was
beginning to look the part too, with buildings that included
classical columns and obelisks, sphinxes and arches, and statues
raised as monumental reminders of the nation's new status and
character. Edinburgh's association with philosophy, neoclassical
architecture and topographical similarities to the Greek city
earned it the nickname 'Athens of the North' – a more suitable
nickname, Edinburghers believed, than 'Auld Reekie'. This was
gentrification, regency style. But a lust for profit lay behind the
facade, and something of the original spark of the Enlightenment
was lost. They did not know it, but the Scottish capital would
never again rise to the global prominence it now revelled in.

At the time, nothing could seem further from the truth,
especially as the high chief of the rebranding efforts was the
novelist, historian and global celebrity Sir Walter Scott. Today,
Scott has joined the ranks of the 'great unread', with his writing style often considered archaic and difficult to follow, but he
was the best-selling author of his day. His influence lives on in
famous tales of Robert the Bruce and the Spider, of Arthur and

the Lady of the Lake, of noble Jacobite warriors and tangled webs that we ought not to weave. It can also be seen in huge memorials erected across Scotland and the world, most notably the Scott Monument on Edinburgh's Princes Street and the central column in Glasgow's George Square.

Perhaps even deeper-rooted than this, Scott led very practical efforts to reimagine Scotland's past following its condemnation as intolerant and barbaric by prominent Scots in the eighteenth century. Scott popularised tartan and the kilt among lowlanders after George IV's state visit in 1822, and led a search party through the neglected Edinburgh Castle in 1818 to rediscover the Crown Jewels of Scotland – the most ancient in Britain. We can also thank Scott for leading the charge in the rehabilitation of Scotland's medieval past, without which Scotland's ancient monuments might have been allowed to fall into further ruin. Scott did not seek a return to a medieval way of life, but he admired values of honour, integrity and sufficiency, which he regarded as heavily corrupted in his own time.

Scott rather less romantically claimed that his native country was a land of lawyers: having originally trained as one himself, he observed, with a hint of despair, that 'the Scottish seem to conceive Themis [Ancient Greek deity of Law] the most powerful of goddesses'. One day Scott would require her divine intervention.

However, it was not among the classical structures of the New Town but by the harbour at Leith that the answer to Scott's prayers would take shape. Born in 1796, John Gibson was the only son of a modest Leith merchant, George Gibson, and his wife Isabella Gibson, the daughter of a shipmaster. John Gibson was at first enrolled in the Kirk parish school by the docks, one of several hundred such schools, which John Davidson had championed in the previous century. The parish schools were among the first instances in the world of a universal free education system. However, with a severe reputation for dishing out the belt in dour surroundings, these schools provided a basic (and short) education, drilling grammar and numeracy into generations of young Scots alongside the virtues of the Presbyterian faith.

Gibson was able to continue his education after the parish school as his family managed to accrue sufficient funds to secure him a place at the Edinburgh High School following some business success. Without their increased income, it is likely Gibson would have served as an apprentice to his father, but instead he had the opportunity to carve out a more privileged role in society than his forebears. Even with his extended education, his comparatively modest origins still placed him at a disadvantage, both socially and politically. Not being established in Edinburgh, he was regarded as an outsider, lacking the family ties to bring him into the grand rooms of the capital or gain him clout in matters of local government. Nonetheless, within just a few years, Gibson would be included among the few individuals entitled not only to vote in city elections, but also to have a say in the infamously restricted parliamentary elections.

This change of fortune did not come easily. After finishing his secondary education, Gibson and his family experienced a rapid decline in their fleeting fortunes as a result of the continental trade blockade of the Napoleonic Wars. Unlike his peers, Gibson had the means to subsist but nothing more. This was made all the more permanent by the premature death of his father at the age of 50. With the family having fallen on desperately hard times, they were forced to bury George Gibson in an unmarked sailor's grave at Leith South Parish Church.

Picking himself up from this personal, and financial, change in fortunes, Gibson managed to gain admittance to the University of Edinburgh. He studied Humanity and Greek in his first year, but soon took up the more vocational study of law, with an apprenticeship under John Nairn concurrent with his studies. Now aged 18, his jet black hair was already receding at the temples and the 'mutton chops' which would encircle his face for the remainder of his life were beginning to take form. An unusual bundle of receipts found in one of the chests reveal that, while completing his studies under Professor David Hume, nephew of the philosopher of the same name, Gibson tried, and failed, to learn the flute. They also show that he purchased various tartan fabrics to make up an assortment of clothes. Sadly, none of these garish delights survive, but the image of the young student in budget tartan trews trying, and failing, to master the flute is compelling.

Five years after his entry to university, Gibson successfully completed his studies and apprenticeship, and was enrolled as a member of the Society of Writers to the Signet. Gibson sought employment among the many legal businesses scattered throughout regency Edinburgh. With no apparent family connections to secure him a post, the young lawyer found work as a Parliament House clerk to Hay Donaldson WS – one of the successors of John Davidson – with clients such as Sir Walter Scott and the infant Duke of Buccleuch.

It was as Donaldson's clerk that Gibson was introduced to Sir Walter Scott. Many years later, when what little hair he had was white, Gibson wrote a short volume, *Reminiscences of Sir Walter Scott*, telling of his association with the famed and eccentric author. Beginning his story, he wrote 'I am now the only survivor of those who were intimately connected with Sir Walter's affairs during the last ten or twelve years of his life, and as I had more opportunities than any other person of observing the noble exertions he made for the benefit of those whom he had unwittingly involved in his misfortunes, I can, on these matters, speak with some authority.' This is the story he had to tell.

As alluded to, Gibson first met Scott through his old master Hay Donaldson, who was Scott's law agent and 'one of Sir

Walter Scott's intimate friends'. This friendship is evident in historical records: Scott successfully proposed Donaldson as a Fellow of the Royal Society of Edinburgh. This intimacy did not extend to the world of business: Scott had secretly become a partner in the printing house of his childhood friend James Ballantyne without Donaldson's knowledge.

Talented though he was as both author and historian, Scott's skills proved insufficient in the world of business. The printers, though prospering at the time of Scott's initial involvement, became hugely unstable following dubious agreements with Scott's publisher Constable, and by 1812 the business was losing £1,000 a year.

In 1823, Hay Donaldson died at a relatively young age following a long and debilitating illness. In one of his last letters, he recommended Gibson to both the Duke of Buccleuch and Scott as his successor as law agent. Following enquiries into his character both clients accepted Donaldson's recommendation, and Gibson inherited the practice at Charlotte Street. Having previously lived in modest accommodation near Leith Docks, Gibson took up residence in the stylish New Town. Despite this change in fortune, he could do anything but rest on his laurels. The young Gibson, still under 30, had to become trustee, literary agent, legal advisor, money lender and estate agent to the best-selling author in the world.

Promptly after Donaldson's death, Gibson was therefore summoned to Abbotsford, Scott's eccentric baronial mansion in the Scottish Borders, dubbed the 'Conundrum Castle'. After a few bumpy hours travelling by horse-drawn carriage, Gibson arrived at the internationally famous home, a visit we might envisage today as comparable to visiting the Caribbean retreat of a reclusive musician nearing the height of their fame. When he arrived he was invited to the author's study, where he noted the table covered in books on the Isle of Man, the location of Scott's next novel, and the secret staircases to the gallery above through which Scott could make an escape from an unwanted visitor. No such evasion was needed on this occasion, as Scott warmly welcomed the 29-year-old and invited him to join his family for an evening of entertainment.

Over time they became closer and formed a bond of trust, with Scott going so far as to allude to his authorship of the Waverley novels – which he had written under a pseudonym – to the young lawyer by personally sending him a copy of the newest edition 'from the Author'. The two regularly paid each other visits, with Scott's Edinburgh house at 39–43 North Castle Street and Gibson living at 23 Lyndoch Place at the western end of the New Town.

Unknown to Gibson, Scott's seemingly endless fortune, expressed through exorbitant spending on parties, artifacts and Abbotsford, concealed a swelling mountain of debt for which he was liable as a partner in James Ballantyne's printers. In 1825/6, the edifice came crashing down as Ballantyne declared bankruptcy and the business was dissolved, saddling Scott with over £120,000 of debt.

To understand the financial predicament that Scott faced four years after Gibson's first visit to Abbotsford, we must recognise how much £120,889 5s 6d was worth in 1826. It is difficult to translate figures such as this into today's monetary value, not only because of the inflation of currency value, but more importantly because of the amount at which commodities and labour were valued. For example, although this figure roughly translates to £10.5 million in 2018, Scott, as the best-selling author of the day, could only hope to make the modern equivalent of £500,000 to £1,500,000 per best-seller, meaning he required around a dozen best-sellers to pay off the debt without factoring in his regular expenses. This was also complicated by the widespread piracy of novels: Scott was widely read in the United States but did not earn a dime in royalties owing to irregular copyright laws. When trying to explain the huge size of this debt, Dr Robert Alloo, great-great-great-grandson of Gibson and the author of *In the Warmth of the Limelight: The Unlikely Partnership of Sir Walter Scott and John Gibson, WS*, described it as 'insurmountable'.

So, with a seriously substantial debt now weighing on Scott, he was presented with three solutions by Gibson. The first was to declare bankruptcy, which Scott ruled out not only because of the public humiliation it represented, but also because he claimed he did not wish others to suffer as a result of his own misfortune. The second option, owing to his fame, was to accept the many forthcoming offers of financial assistance from wealthy patrons, possibly including King George IV. But Scott was determined to dig himself out of this hole by his own efforts. The third and most arduous option was the one to which Gibson and Scott agreed – the creation of a trust to manage Scott's expenses and income, with the chief purpose of gradually paying off creditors through sale of assets and revenue from new works.

Scott was reluctantly on board, but requested that John Gibson sit as the sole trustee, an arrangement Gibson felt would constitute a severe conflict of interest. As such, Gibson persuaded Scott that he would instead serve as the senior trustee, with two other trustees approved by the Bank of Scotland and Sir William Forbes & Co., an important creditor. This strategy also necessitated a dramatic shift in Scott's position on the authorship of the Waverley novels: he had to move from anonymity to open authorship both to assure the creditors of his ability to repay his debts and to increase the potential revenue from future works. Again, Scott reluctantly agreed, and in doing so made a start on the long road to financial recovery.

The Trust's first act was the implementation of sweeping austerity. On close examination of Scott's poorly kept accounts, it was clear that easy savings could be made by dramatically reducing Scott's spending on entertainment and suspending the incessant improvements carried out on his Abbotsford Estate. A little starker perhaps was the decision to sell Scott's townhouse on Edinburgh's Castle Street. This came with a degree of public humiliation, as what was once Scott's drawing room was converted into a makeshift auction house to sell off the house's furniture piece by piece. Gibson participated in the auction too, buying a dining table (among other items) for his home. On later visits to Gibson's house, Scott would note, in an apparently neutral tone, that much of the furniture had formerly belonged to him. Certain items even made their way into Gibson's Charlotte Street offices, though they have now passed into collections such as the Writers' Museum, Edinburgh.

After Scott's departure from Edinburgh and the restriction of his celebrity lifestyle, his literary output increased substantially: between 1826 and 1832 he produced six novels, two short stories, two plays, eleven historical volumes and a journal, in addition to several unfinished works. These included *Woodstock, Chronicles of the Canongate, Tales of a Grandfather, Castle Dangerous* as well as a *History of Scotland* and the biographical *Life of Napoleon*. The last of these brought him into frequent correspondence with the Duke of Wellington, then the British Prime Minister, keeping him in the limelight of elite society – something the Trust encouraged and accommodated financially. Anecdotally, Gibson recounted that 'during this period on one occasion [Scott] added he had no fears of his works finding a ready sale, "for since poor Byron died, there is no one whose works the publishers care so much for as my own". I am not quite sure if he did not say "care for *but* my own". I rather think he did.'

In the adversity and hardship of these times, Scott and Gibson grew closer. At Lady Scott's funeral in 1826, Gibson was asked to make all the arrangements on behalf of Sir Walter Scott, and was drawn into the family's inner circle. After the sale of his house in Edinburgh, Scott often stayed with the Gibsons, though eventually he was forced to become a lodger for longer durations of stay. On one occasion when Mrs Gibson invited Scott to dine with the family during a visit, he responded 'Oh yes, I am coming back for dinner, but just let me go about the house as a tame cat.' With the Trust controlling Scott's allowances, he also relied upon Gibson personally for small loans, often in the region of £50, to make visits to London to advance his historical research and maintain his fame. In addition, Scott often 'forwarded' to Gibson old women asking for charity, requesting that he offer them support, such a frequent occurrence that Scott once wrote to Gibson 'You will think I am sending all the widows in the country to you.' The two would also discuss Scott's health, which had been fragile since he was a boy, a major concern for the Trust as the payment of debts relied on the long life of Sir Walter Scott.

Around this time, Gibson along with several other Writers to the Signet probably attended the Christmas Eve trial of the bodysnatcher and murderer William Burke at Parliament House. Gibson and Scott discussed the event with great interest in correspondence, with Scott in particular sceptical of the innocence of Dr Knox, who had bought the bodies from Burke and Hare. The bloody conclusion of this national horror was attended by both Scott and Gibson, along with 25,000 other onlookers, when Burke was publicly executed in 1829. As Scott's confidence grew on the back of the success of his increased literary output, the Trust decided to reward his rapid recuperation of the creditors' debts by moving to a less austere regime. Scott credited Gibson with this, who as Scott's de facto literary agent was responsible for achieving sales previously unheard of in Britain. Among the first, and largest, of these sales was *Woodstock*, to which Gibson sold the rights for the sensational sum of £26,000. Upon hearing the news, Scott responded with elation, 'my dear sir, you have made a glorious sale!'. *Life of Napoleon*, written in several volumes, also fetched a considerable sum through Gibson's negotiations. The work ethic of the two cannot be understated, as Gibson simultaneously acted for the Duke of Buccleuch and many other private clients while negotiating the sale of the best-selling books of the best-selling author in the world.

Nonetheless, with such a mountain of debt still to clear, and many fearing that the ageing Scott would not be able to continue at such a pace forever, issues regarding the ownership of Scott's work were dredged up by creditors. Some claimed that they should cut out the middleman and directly own whatever Scott wrote the moment it left his quill until the debt was cleared. In short, the old man would be converted into a cash cow, lacking the dignity of the ownership of his work.

Unsurprisingly, Gibson fought ferociously against this proposition in what would become a watershed moment in the development of intellectual property in Scotland. This was new ground, not only in Scotland but in Britain as a whole: as Gibson observed, 'no similar question had ever been raised in any court of law wither in England or Scotland'. The real crux of the issue was that Constable, Scott's current publisher and a creditor, owned part of the publishing rights to future works because of advances paid to Scott, though this relied on the agreement that authorship would remain anonymous. As Scott had been forced to reveal his identity, he considered all future publications as inapplicable to this agreement. Scott would not put up with the situation whereby he was effectively indentured to write new works for Constable until his death, writing to Gibson that Constable had 'no more right [to my work] than Burke and Hare had to daft Tam's body'.

Gibson responded to Scott's fears swiftly, and put the question to Scotland's legal system. Before the judge Lord Newton, it was argued that Scott's works were unquantifiable items up until the moment they were sold, with the previous agreement broken at the point of the revelation of authorship. A portion of proceeds, not the books themselves, would be paid to the creditors. The key ingredient to this argument was reason, which the Enlightenment had offered Scotland's judicial system to plug the gaps in its archaic legal codes, and evidently it was enough. Thanks to this case and argument, in 1827 Lord Newton ruled that Scott was allowed to retain his books. Nevertheless, a 'triangle' of responsibility for published works would be formed with the Trust, Scott and his new publisher – Robert Cadell. While a victory for the future of Scots law, this decision had a fatal flaw for Scott. The newly empowered publisher, Cadell, was the nephew of the hated creditor Constable and would tirelessly strive to tear apart the Trust for his own financial gain, driving Scott into overdrive, and ultimately an early grave.

As Cadell gradually took greater control of Scott's literary career, spurring the author on to further projects on tighter timescales, Scott's energy turned to exhaustion. By the early 1830s the concern for Scott's health was so great that the Trust agreed to fund a trip to Italy for his recuperation. He travelled to Italy aboard a steamer, largely bound to a wheelchair. Scott's health appeared to improve initially in Italy, but soon fell back to its alarmingly fragile state upon his return. His finances were also not as robust as he believed: given his huge output of work over the past several years, he had started to delude himself that his debt, still in the region of £73,000, was nearly paid off.

Near the end of his life, Scott began to lose some of the extraordinary mental powers he was known for, and in response turned against formerly close family and friends. The possible deterioration of his intellectual capacity had always frightened Scott, and in one letter to Gibson he had described senility as a fate worse than death. Gibson eventually found himself on the receiving end of Scott's mental deterioration when a disagreement concerning the state of the finances drove a wedge between the two. Scott increasingly relied instead upon his publisher Robert Cadell, who encouraged the fantasy that his finances were now back to good health, all the while accruing huge wealth from the sale of Scott's final works.

As Scott's death gradually grew nearer, he reconciled with Gibson, and the family relied heavily upon the loyalty of the young lawyer. On 21 September 1832, Sir Walter Scott's vast energies finally gave out and he died at Abbotsford. A week later, as he had planned to the letter, Scott's funeral proved to be a spectacular display of Scotland's past, with a funeral

---

12 Charlotte Street
(office of John Gibson, later Strathern & Blair)

12 Charlotte Street served as a base for legal practice for 200 years, starting with John Davidson's successor John Home, then John Gibson, Strathern & Blair and eventually Anderson Strathern. It was graced by Sir Walter Scott, prime ministers and aristocrats. Through the wall from Gibson's office was the birthplace and childhood home of Alexander Graham Bell. It is possible he lived in one of the flats owned by the firm, which surrounded the office; if so, he was fortunate as the rent remained fixed from 1826 to 1901. During the Second World War, when most of the lawyers in the practice were serving in the war, the women and elderly partners of Strathern & Blair successfully sustained the business in a challenging environment. As a precautionary measure against incendiary bombs, they took the unusual step of encasing confidential documents inside the framework of the walls. After the end of the war these documents were forgotten, only to be uncovered decades later during renovation work. Following the merger of Strathern & Blair and J&F Anderson in 1992 the offices continued to be home to several departments of the new Anderson Strathern, but the rapid expansion of the newly merged firm demanded that operations be placed under one roof. The building was finally vacated in 1999.

Bust of John Gibson in the Signet Library,
Parliament Square, Edinburgh.

procession over a mile long following his casket to Dryburgh Abbey. Gibson was also in attendance and was invited to Abbotsford to be part of an intimate family dinner after the funeral. Years before, Scott had written in *Ivanhoe* on the subject of death, 'Is death the last sleep? No, it is the last final awakening.'

Some of Scott's final words seem to have brought comfort to Gibson during this time: near his death when encouraged to pep up with his favourite phrase 'Time and I against any two', he responded 'vain boast!'. The veil of Scott's vanity had been lifted, and Gibson was reconciled with the author. Indeed, while Scott's ambition had complicated his financial and social relations, Gibson admired that it never interfered with his integrity. Scott represented a supportive, albeit complicated, father figure to Gibson at the end – a role Gibson had almost always found lacking, given the deaths in his formative years of both his father and his mentor, Hay Donaldson. Long after his death, Scott held a privileged place in the heart and mind of John Gibson.

It took sixteen years after Scott's death to finally clear the author's debts, but following his expressed wishes, no individual came off the worse for his mistake. However, this long afterlife of Scott's patronage was background to Gibson's main work of expanding and enhancing his practice. With an eye towards specialising in private representation of the elite of Scottish society, Gibson took on several apprentices, and eventually partners, who operated from the Charlotte Street office. These included his son Henry Gordon Gibson, John Home (a grandson of John Home, the apprentice and clerk of John Davidson) as well as Robert Strathern, the partner to whom Anderson Strathern owes part of its name.

A great deal of Gibson's time was now devoted to managing the affairs of the 5th Duke of Buccleuch. While still wrapping up the financial affairs of the late Scott, from 1837 Gibson was engaged in the more creative task of assisting in the duke's project to dramatically extend Edinburgh's Granton Harbour. To this day, the huge plans and maps relating to this massive task are held by Anderson Strathern; not only was a fully functional steamship harbour constructed, but also rail terminals, housing for workers, warehouses and public services such as schools. We might imagine that, given his upbringing on Leith Docks, Gibson would have had the emotional connection and personal experience to help drive the Granton Harbour project to completion, and assist Buccleuch in delivering a very early example of an industrial project built to serve the community and the individual. Coincidentally the opening of the harbour was set on the same day as the coronation of Queen Victoria. With the Duke of Buccleuch, the bearer of the Golden Staff for the Queen, in attendance in London, Gibson became responsible for presiding over the official opening ceremony, becoming publicly associated with the project.

When the final stage of construction of Granton Harbour was completed in 1842, the young Queen Victoria arrived by its jetty for her first visit to Scotland. Opening the east of Scotland to the new ships and transport of the steam age, the new harbour triggered a wave of industrialisation, including the construction of a quarry, which provided the material for Nelson's Column in Trafalgar Square. These constructions also spurred Gibson to help another client, Captain Sir Sam Brown, to submit plans for a bridge across the Firth of Forth. Brown's plan, made in the 1840s, was a huge influence on the final design of the iconic Forth Rail Bridge, now a UNESCO World Heritage Site.

The people of Edinburgh erected a statue of the duke in West Parliament Square in the heart of the Old Town. A window of the Signet Library, partly founded by John Davidson, looks out onto this square. Gazing out from this window is a bust of Gibson, his mutton chops rendered in white marble.

During this time, Gibson and his family lived on the duke's Dalkeith Estate in a large and comfortable house, an arrangement of convenience that provided a familiarity on a personal level between Gibson and the duke. The business relationship also took on another dimension as Gibson advised the duke on political matters. One letter from the duke asked Gibson for his legal advice on the implementation of an income tax as proposed by the Peel government. In response, Gibson reserved comment on the issue until the specifics were established.

In later life, Gibson continued to have brushes with fame, most notably in his frequent encounters with Queen Victoria and Prince Albert during their visits to Scotland. Though it is unclear what occurred at these meetings, they must have been a success, as at some point before his death Prince Albert

Guide to Queen Victoria's Coronation (1838)

This guide, which probably belonged to a historical partner of Bell & Scott, details the proceedings and events on the day of the coronation of Queen Victoria. While the booklet suggests the coronation would proceed with dignified ceremony, the event itself proved to be shambolic. Victoria was told her movements only moments before the ceremony began, and those around her had not bothered to rehearse their roles, leading to widespread improvisation. At points the five-hour ceremony became so tedious that the royal party got up and ceremoniously entered St Stephen's Chapel (the most sacred location in Westminster Abbey) to take a break at the altar, which according to Lord Melbourne, a close friend and adviser to the queen, was 'covered with plates of sandwiches, bottles of wine, etc.'. Only four coronations have been held since Queen Victoria's, so we can only speculate if this regal tradition of a finger buffet has been passed down the ages. Along with the guide are tickets to the slightly less disastrous coronation of Victoria's uncle William IV.

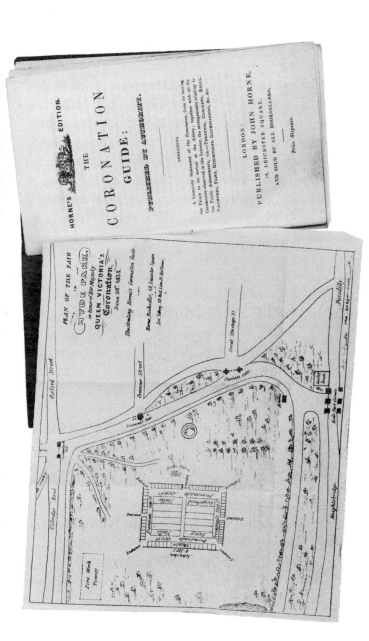

A pamphlet of the coronation of Queen Victoria, 1838.

initiated Gibson into the Order of Albert for services to Saxony – a highly unusual move as the order was generally reserved for Saxon citizens. The bust of Gibson at the Signet Library features a likeness of the associated medal.

Later in his career, Gibson and partner John Home worked extensively for the scientist Andrew Combe, one of Britain's most eminent physicians and the founder of the pseudoscience of phrenology. Experimenting on the human brain, Combe sought to understand mental abnormalities based on bumps in the skull, with perhaps his most famous creation a map of the human mind, compartmentalised into different desires and impulses. He died very young, and documents relating to his research into the human psyche, brain and spirit made their way into the archives of the firm. Another client and naturalist, Sir William Jardine, similarly left his collection of scientific papers to Gibson, among which are some of the first sketches of exotic animals such as the duck-billed platypus. Perhaps in Gibson they found a fellow enthusiast, with Gibson collecting samples of unusual geologic formations as well as ancient axe-heads from across the world, now all held at the National Museum of Scotland.

Following the death of his son and partner Henry Gordon Gibson, Gibson resigned his treasurership of the WS Society and devoted his old age to the support of his son's young family. His son's death had followed the premature death of another partner, William Home, son of John Home, who died of health problems connected to alcoholism at the age of 50. William Home's personal diary is held at the NRS and would shed further light on his life.

In his eighties Gibson was still working full-time at Charlotte Street and was doing a great deal of work for the Duke of Buccleuch and other clients. His young partner Robert Strathern, who was made partner in 1872, was gradually taking on greater responsibility, but it was still clear that

A lock of hair from Lady Sophia Hastings, 1818

An unusual item found among the collection of Alexander Duncan and his successors was a lock of hair belonging to Lady Sophia Hastings, the mother of the 3rd Marquess of Bute. Lady Sophia was the daughter of the Earl of Moira, Governor-General of India, and the Countess of Loudoun. Her family was struck by tragedy in her youth as her sister, Lady Flora, a lady-in-waiting to Queen Victoria, found herself mired in scandal at court. She was suspected to be pregnant, and following an onslaught by the popular press, and an expulsion from court, the famously prudish queen demanded she be examined medically to confirm the rumours. The examination discovered that Flora was suffering from a large tumour and, a few months later, exonerated by a shamed press, she died. Lady Sophia herself would also die of Bright's disease at the age of 50, with her 12-year-old son, the 3rd Marquess of Bute and future client of J&F Anderson, at her bedside. She was described by the minister officiating at her funeral as 'one firm, yet gentle, loving and wise'. Her son would go on to argue for complete Catholic emancipation, construct Mount Stuart on the Isle of Bute, the first private million-pound home, and build Bute Hall, the centrepiece of the main building of the University of Glasgow.

Small lock of blonde hair belonging to Lady Sophia
Hastings, dated 1818.

the old man was in charge. Finally, after over fifty-five years at the helm, Gibson relinquished his senior partnership of the firm to Strathern, dying just one month after his departure.

Gibson's legacy goes beyond his mutton-chopped bust; it is tangible to us in the legal and the physical landscape of Scotland. As a stepping stone between the Enlightenment and modernity, Gibson encapsulated the benefits of a rational and utilitarian view of law, whether in the expansion of Edinburgh at Granton Harbour or his contribution to the creation of intellectual property rights. He was defined by an industrious and persistent work ethic the strength of which steadily moved him from relative poverty to royal circles. This kind of meritocratic advancement would become increasingly rare in the century that followed. Sir Walter Scott died many years before his young solicitor friend, but I suspect his words remained with Gibson to the end: 'A lawyer without history or literature is a mechanic, a mere working mason; if he possesses some knowledge of these, he may venture to call himself an architect.'

5

Victorian Practices: John Inglis and Alexander Stevenson Blair

'I told him I was an atheist and he seemed rather shocked at the announcement'

Despite the Scottish Enlightenment having had a more egalitarian spirit than those of France and Germany, by the middle of the nineteenth century, doors were again closing to talented individuals of humble origins. The first hints of a meritocracy, albeit one exclusive to a small section of society, had allowed for the rise of remarkable individuals such as John Davidson and John Gibson. But as the middle and upper class swelled in numbers, limited professional positions became monopolised: those who had risen during this period of relative relaxation entrenched their positions for the next generation. The law entered an era defined by class and moral panic, with sour stooges and stiff-collared socialites aplenty.

The legal practices of J&F Anderson in Castle Street (established by Thomas Cranstoun in 1793) and Strathern & Blair in Charlotte Street, now occupied by their august Victorian occupants, at times fell into the realms of the Dickensian. Both offices were under the firm control of doorkeepers, who maintained the properties and lived on site in spacious apartments either at street level or on the top floor. Through much of the nineteenth century, Castle Street is said to have been 'under the domestic charge of a very ancient and very cantankerous, if very faithful, old servant who was in a chronic condition of conflict with the junior clerks of the establishment'. Such doorkeepers, who tended the coal fires and kept the offices well looked after, often remained with the firms over several decades; this tradition lasted into the 1980s. During this time and beyond, both firms acted for the aristocracy as well as the intellectual and artistic elite of Scotland.

It would be a mistake to assume that the firms were exclusively preoccupied by the business of international writers, aristocrats and the Crown. As is seen in one letter, the writer and client George Farquharson required assistance with a more personal matter:

Dear Sir,

As I have already received so much impertinence not to call insolence from Mr Moncur about the completion of the Water Closet here, I beg you will use all means as will force him to get it finished without more delay – it is now considerably more than a month since it was begun and at the present rate of proceeding it may be another month before it is done – and as my agreement to raise my offer was entirely on condition of getting that convenience, I have much cause to complaint to Mr Moncur, especially [as] I know that ten days was amply sufficient to have completed the whole. It is also a very serious grievance to me not having it finished. I beg you will therefore not lose an hour in applying to Moncur over the subject.

Yours truly,

George Farquharson

Friday, 17th June 1836

Dirty business was also occurring within the office: on several occasions clerks hatched criminal plans to run away with the family silver. While most schemes were foiled, in one case an unnamed young clerk made away with the stamp money kept at the Castle Street office. In the later, dishevelled account of the episode, we are told the partners at the firm caught on to the plot just an hour after they had seen the clerk leave the office. Immediately, they despatched a party along the Great North Road to chase down the suspect before he made his way south of the border and beyond. Despite the coach travelling at full gallop through the night, the young clerk managed to escape the clutches of his pursuers aboard 'a barque from Newcastle to the West Indies'. He was never seen or heard of again.

The Victorian stereotypes, so potent in the popular imagination, seem to be confirmed. But just a short walk from John Gibson's office in Charlotte Street, we find signs of an anti-establishment, revolutionary swelling of ideas behind the door of 48 Castle Street. A diary of a clerk, John Inglis, allows us to creak open the weighty black door of that building, for 200 years the home of J&F Anderson, to walk its corridors and reimagine the ideas of those not fortunate enough to have their name above the door. Inglis was far from the Bob Cratchit cliché of a meek and downtrodden lackey, but rather a passionate environmentalist, vegetarian, atheist and socialist, someone who today could easily be imagined protesting against ecological destruction, or gracing some of the finest avant-garde vegan bistros the city had to offer.

From the few surviving descriptions of Inglis, at the time of writing his diary he was a short, wiry man in his early thirties, with a neat brown moustache and gentle face. As with most men of the period, he wore a suit and tie for almost every occasion – regular wear having banished the original creases. Upon examining the Castle Street ledgers, we find Inglis earned a fixed salary of £120 per annum, triple the national average, and

48 Castle Street (office of J&F Anderson)

This building was contracted to be constructed in 1793 by Thomas Cranstoun, who operated contemporaneously to John Davidson, in the fashionable New Town. While maintaining his link to the Old Town through the building's views of the castle and the now drained Nor Loch (today's Princes Street Gardens), it was the eighteenth-century equivalent of a sleek and modern glass skyscraper, albeit also Cranstoun's home. The masons commissioned to construct the building, the Williamson brothers, later went on to build the White House in Washington DC. Over time, the premises expanded into No. 50 which, in 1884, had its entrance sealed up, and over the next century the practice would continue to grow to cover nearly half of Castle Street.

John Inglis, the firm's chief clerk in the late Victorian era, worked in this building and recalled how cold its old walls could become during the depths of winter. And in *Random Recollections* by James Bland Sutherland it was also noted that, even when gas lighting was commonly available, the offices were still lit by candlelight. This would not matter to John Anderson, the senior partner of the firm at the time, as he was almost totally blind and had to have letters dictated to him. Anderson was described by Sutherland as 'one of the best and most sagacious men of business I ever came into contact with' with 'perfect integrity and sense of honour'.

This office was retained by the firm until 2004, at which point larger, more open premises were required following the merger with Strathern & Blair, ending 211 years of continuous occupation.

managed to live a comparatively prosperous life in the Dean Village with his wife, Teen, and son. On a day-to-day basis, Inglis was tasked with balancing the books of the firm, collecting feu duties across Scotland and generally helping around the business, for example translating letters from French to

PLATE I. Copy of a Heritable Bond from the reign of James IV, written in Scots (1505).

Whitehall. 6. Decemb.r 1681.

Deare Brother.

I am very glad to heare, you are so well able to vndertake a
Iourny to Drogheda, and to Dublin, & yo.r Sonne Arthur likes S.r
James Grahams Daughter, I think, they haue no reason to make
difficultys, or exceptions to what you propose,
The Drafte which M.r Farewell hath sent me, shall be dispatcht
to morrow, the King went yesterday to Windsor, and doth not
returne till to morrow night,
I haue acquainted my Cousin Gwin with yo.r Proiect about conceal-
led Lands, and yo.r intention to divide with him, vpon which
account he will be ready to solicit that affaire, when it shall
properly come heere, But it must take its course, and haue its first
Reference to my Lord Lieutenant of Ireland, which I haue transmitted
to you by this soe that you may loose no time, when it returnes
it must be referd to the Lords of the Treasury, before it comes to the
King.
This afternoone my Wife was sworne one of the Ladys of the
Bed Chamber to the Queen.
Our great affaires heere depend vpon removing the force, which the
French vse about Luxembourg, and if it be not removed, it will
certainly necessitate, his Ma.tie to call a Parliam.t

PLATE 2. Letter from Edward, Earl of Conway, to his brother concerning the
Court of Charles II (1681). See Letters of the Law document 2.1.

Be it Known To all Men by these presents,
Me Adam Smith lawfull Son of the deceast Adam Smith
late Comptroller of the Customs at Kirkaldie Now one
of the Professors of Philosophy in the University of Glasgow,
Forasmuchas Mrs Margaret Balfour Widow Daughter
of the deceast Robert Lord Burleigh by her bond dated the
Seventh day of february One Thousand Seven hundred and
Sixty three years Granted her to have Borrowed & Received
at the term of Candlemass then last notwithstanding the
date of the said Bond from the Persons therein named my
Tutors upon Account of me their Pupil, All and whole the
Sum of Four Thousand Merks Scots money, which Sum the
said Mrs Margaret Balfour Bound and obliged her her
heirs Exers and Successors to Content and Repay to me and
my said Tutors on my Account and my heirs or Assignees
at and against the Term of Lambas then next, with the
Sum of Eight hundred Merks money foresaid of liquidate
penalty in case of failzie, Together with the due and ordinary
Rent of the said principall Sum Yearly termly and proportionally so long as the Same should remain unpaid, And for
further Security to me and my foresaids & my said Tutors
anent the premisses, and but hurt or prejudice to the foresaid
personall obligement, The said Mrs Margaret Balfour
Bound and obliged her and her foresaids to Infeft and have
me and my foresaids upon her own proper Charges and
Expences in an Yent of Two hundred Merks or such Rent
as shall Correspond by the Laws of Scotland for the time to
the foresaid principall Sum of Four Thousand Merks Yearly
to be Uplifted and Taken at Two terms in the year, Lambas
& Candlemass by equall Portions forth of All and haill
the Town and Lands of Dempsterton Easter and Wester
Milnland and Skibbland and that part called Walker land
with parks pendicles Annexes Connexes Dependencys Adherents
Just Tennets Tennendries and Services of free Tennents of the
same with all their pertinents, All Lying within the Parish
of Auchtermuchty and Sheriffdome of Fife, and which are
Parts and pertinents of the Barony of Strathmiglo, Or
forth of any part or portion of the saids Lands readiest
Maills

Adam Smith

PLATE 3. Dispensation and Assignation from Adam Smith to Robert Balfour
Ramsay (1754) – see Letters of the Law document 2.3.

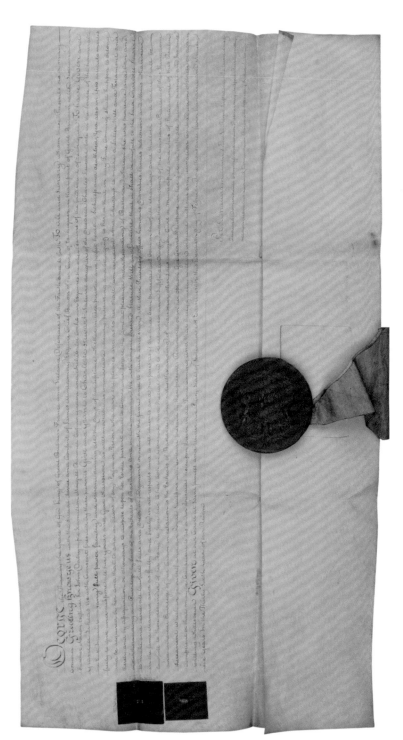

PLATE 4. Legitimisation of Charlotte Stewart under the Privy Seal of George III (1796).

Conversation. Demonstration.

PLATE 5. (*Above*) Portrait of John Davidson (far left) in conversation with Lord Henderland, George Paton, Lord Monboddo and James Hutton (left to right). A monkey can be seen between Monboddo and Hutton, as an expression of Monboddo's theories of the descent of humans from apes (1797).

PLATE 6. (*Left*) John Gibson sitting for a photograph in old age, several decades after his association with Sir Walter Scott (c. 1870).

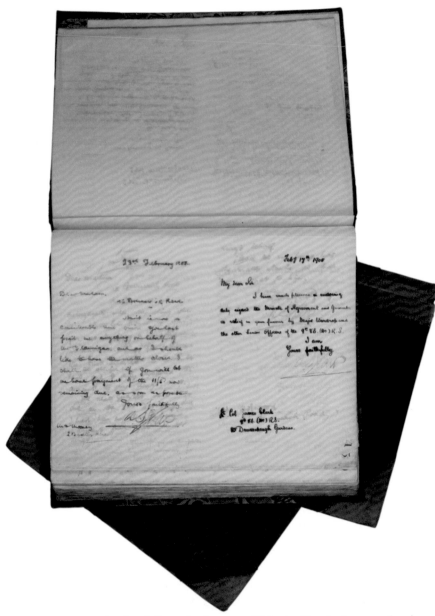

PLATE 7. Letter books of Alexander Stevenson Blair, detailing both personal and private correspondence (1889–1913).

PLATE 8. Cartoon titled 'Lambast of Muir', with Muir (unknown) being hung by representations of justice, virtue, education etc. (nineteenth century).

PLATE 9. Ian Mackenzie, partner at Strathern & Blair, shortly before his death in Djerba, Tunisia, during the North African Campaign (c. 1942).

PLATE 10. Rosemary Mackenzie, secretary at Strathern & Blair, in uniform around the time of her work in Italy with the British Army as a nurse (c. 1944).

PLATE 11. J&F Anderson retirement party for Pat Smyth (bottom row, left) with Douglas Stewart (top row, right) in 1968.

PLATE 12. J&F Anderson Coat of Arms, awarded by the Court of the Lord Lyon (1990), and detailing the history of J&F Anderson from its founding by Thomas Cranstoun in the eighteenth century.

A view of 48 Castle Street in recent times,
the office of J&F Anderson for over 200 years.

English for the junior partner, Frederick Pitman. By and large, given the small size and diverse tasks of the firm, Inglis escaped from the mind-numbing drudgery experienced by the average British office worker, who, as the *Liverpool Daily Post* noted in 1877, was uniquely 'tired of, not with his work'.

The relationship between Inglis and Pitman appears to have been strained, reaching a climax when, on 31 July 1881, Inglis noted with horror that £510 was missing from the accounts. This was a significant amount – more than twelve times the average annual wage in Scotland. The diary entries over the next week are frenetic and brief, but they end with relief as the lost funds are recouped following a scrupulous investigation. The two also worked closely on legal cases across Scotland, with Inglis contributing the brainpower while Pitman would act as the gentlemanly face and mouthpiece of the practice. This strained and grossly unbalanced clerk–partner relationship was common and persisted beyond Inglis and Pitman well into the mid twentieth century. It was also one Inglis had no hope of escaping, as by now a substantial personal wealth was a prerequisite for becoming a partner – John Inglis had climbed as far as he could.

This was not to say that the work was repetitive, or even uninteresting. Certainly clerks were the manpower behind the cases the partners publicly took on; clerks at Castle Street were intricately involved in the investigation of a highly sensationalised murder case. The supposed victim was Edwin Rose, an English visitor to the island of Arran who had disappeared on a hike to the summit of Goatfell in 1889. Following a two-week island-wide search, an islander found the battered remains of the young man, concealed beneath a multitude of boulders below the summit of the peak. As the rocks had been heaved onto the corpse in a manner defying natural explanation, the hunt was on for Rose's killer. John Watson Laurie, a 26-year-old engineer from Glasgow, was the last to be seen with Rose alive.

Tracing the footsteps of the two young men, investigators found that they had met on Bute where they were both holidaying separately. On an excursion to Arran by steamboat, Rose had approached Laurie claiming to recognise his face; the two began talking. They discovered that they both planned to return to Arran to climb Goatfell, the island's highest peak, and so, following this chance meeting, they arranged to remain on the island overnight and tackle Goatfell the following day. Having shared a room the night before, the pair scaled the peak, passing several other hikers en route, though at this point the trail of sightings grows cold. At any rate, Rose was not seen alive again.

This association between Rose and Laurie, along with accounts of Laurie wearing Rose's clothes the day after Rose was last seen, led investigators on a manhunt for John Laurie. After several days, they found Laurie in a quarry in Lanarkshire where he had been hiding since the events on Arran, living on scraps. When he was discovered, he had a razor pressed against his own throat but was unable to make the deadly cut.

By this point, the whole of Britain was gripped in the frenzy of the case, and Pitman was assigned as a prosecutor. Although Laurie's behaviour in the quarry might indicate guilt, Laurie claimed that he had only robbed Rose, not killed him. It was difficult to substantiate this claim, given the complete lack of witnesses or forensic evidence, but the public were baying for blood. The avenue of enquiry into the possibility that the two had been sexually intimate, or that a misunderstanding had turned violent as Rose made an advance on Laurie, was not considered – though in hindsight this seems a likely explanation, given Rose's advances on the steamboat.

With little hard evidence to pin the crime on Laurie, the impatient judge presiding over the trial took Pitman's dubious claims of damning circumstantial evidence at face value, citing the character and reputation of Pitman as a reason for acceptance. By a majority of one, the jury convicted Laurie to be hanged, with the rest supporting the 'not proven' verdict unique to Scots law. It was partly due to this close call, as well as several complaints regarding the process, that led to Laurie eventually having his death sentence replaced with life imprisonment; he continued to plead his innocence until his death 41 years later.

For Inglis and other clerks, day-to-day business was generally less dramatic. In one diary entry, Inglis tells us how he carried out errands across Scotland for Pitman and others, including the collection of feu duties and delivering messages by hand to important clients such as John Crichton-Stuart, 3rd Marquess of Bute. J&F Anderson would also assist Bute in his patronage of the University of Glasgow, including the construction of the graduation hall – Bute Hall – which still stands at the heart of Sir George Gilbert Scott's Gothic masterpiece. Bute later became patron to several other architectural constructions, including his own home at Mount Stuart, which became the world's first privately owned million-pound home. He was also involved in a ground-breaking court case (later overturned) which ruled that the Marquess was not liable in the bankruptcy of the Cardiff Savings Bank (of which he had been a director) as he was six months old when he became a company director and only attended one board meeting in 38 years.

Inglis's radical views were evident in the office. In one diary entry, he describes how his employer was taken aback: 'I told him [Pitman] I was an atheist and he seemed rather shocked at the announcement.' It was indeed shocking at the time: although religious tolerance had increased over recent decades, the tolerance was of different interpretations of God, not complete denial. In this staunchly religious society, God was the source of morality, so to deny his existence was to deny any difference between right and wrong. As Inglis was the man in charge of the money, we can imagine that such statements would have raised a few nervous eyebrows. On one occasion, the clerk also prompted fury as he tossed a Bible into a fire in retaliation for his protective aunt burning a bundle of his socialist pamphlets. This exchange seriously upset his wife Teen as she was the devout daughter of a Catholic missionary who was at the time converting communities across the Empire. Nonetheless, it is clear from Inglis's concern for the poor, the environment and other good causes that his life stood as testament against fears of atheism encouraging an amoral life.

Unlike the serious concern about his religious convictions felt by those around him, his vocal vegetarianism was taken more lightly, with the young Archie Pitman teasing the clerk mercilessly over his unorthodox diet. Inglis did eat fish on a Friday, as was traditional, and consumed an inordinate quantity of oysters, but other than this he appears to have strictly adhered to a vegetarian diet. He also appears to have abstained from alcohol, another faux pas within legal circles at the time. Inglis appears to have been quite a divisive, if placid character. Significantly, he could never be accused of looking down on others.

Though a radical liberal in his day, John Inglis would perhaps now be more accurately described as a socialist. Politically, he seems to have been comfortable to support establishment politicians: he was an enthusiastic supporter of Gladstone, the four-time Liberal Prime Minister and MP for nearby Midlothian. Nonetheless, the revolutionary in him awoke as he read the writings of his contemporary Karl Marx, noting in his diary 'Mr Dow told us about the rows in the shops between the capitalist and the labourers, and the meanness the men had to submit to at the hands of the master.' Office workers of the world unite! Thankfully for Inglis, this was not his first-hand experience, as his own work afforded him the flexibility and means to attend lectures and other events in the city and entertain a variety of distantly related foreign visitors at his home.

Indeed, most days he worked only from 10am to 4pm and could expect his wife to cover all household duties. Occasionally, he and Teen would also take trips to the Highlands with their baby, who is only ever referred to as 'the boy'. Here, however, Inglis reached the limits of his resources: he and those like him were unable to indulge in travel beyond Scotland's borders as the Anderson and Pitman partners would have done. Inglis's curiosity about lands further afield could only be realised through photographs of distant lands and people, which he bought at specialist shops in the New Town and later traded with others in the office.

The laissez-faire approach to running an office went both ways. As stated, although the Andersons and later the Pitman family owned and technically ran the business, clerks such as Inglis invariably did the bulk of the legal work behind the scenes. At times this resulted in clerks, including Inglis, working beyond two o'clock in the morning to complete urgent work, with the Pitmans checking-in via carriage as they travelled from one soirée to another.

Although many of the issues Inglis felt passionate about have only recently entered the mainstream, he regarded himself as living through the crunch point of the political, religious and environmental upheavals he felt so passionately about. For example, Inglis writes with excitement about 'a Norwegian anticipation in regard to utilising the heat of the Sun for purposes for manufacture when the supply of coal gives out' – what we today would call solar power. Similarly, his excitement regarding 'the proposed tunnel between France and England below the English Channel' would remain a pipe dream for decades to come. Other scientific beliefs – such as the potential to harness the gravitational pull of the planets to generate electricity – may yet be ahead of even our own time. Inglis did, nevertheless, witness great innovation. In a diary entry from 1881, he describes with awe the installation of electrified streetlamps on Princes Street (a step too far in the opinion of some, who warned that the intense lights would blind pedestrians). Who would expect to find the fear of 'the Elephant becoming an extinct animal' in a Victorian clerk's diary? Inglis stands as a prime example of the fact that issues we might believe to have surfaced only recently have actually been grappled with for many generations.

Tragically the diary ends on 13 October 1881 without fanfare, with the brief note 'Been a fine day although rather cold.' Shortly fterwards, John was struck down with typhoid fever from which he did not recover, dying at the young age, even for then, of 42. His remaining family blamed 'eating oysters, of which he was inordinately fond'. It seems John Inglis lived an engaging and active, if short, life, propelled by a strong desire for self-improvement and, as a result, the improvement of the society in which he lived. Teen lived much longer than her husband, dying at the age of 92. She was buried next to John at Morningside cemetery.

As ever, the ancient firms strove on, replacing those lost to death or retirement with others. The owners also changed with the passing of time: the Andersons were replaced by the Pitmans at J&F Anderson, and the Gibsons by the Blairs at the future Strathern & Blair. Before Alexander Stevenson Blair joined the firm in 1891, Robert Strathern, to whom the current firm owes its name, had operated alone since the death of John Gibson in 1877. This is a crucial juncture, as it was the last point that either of the firms was composed of a sole partner, and the point at which Strathern & Blair's name would solidify around those two names, with no more changes for over a century. This was necessary as the rapid turnaround in the name above the door was becoming a problem; it diluted the reputation of such old practices, and would eventually become untenable as the number of partners dramatically increased in the twentieth century. Compared with earlier chapters, we grapple with an era rather than an individual.

Robert Strathern would come to have a far more meaningful legacy than his name alone. Like Gibson, Strathern set precedents in the law that last to this day, and have only gained relevance with time. Strathern was the first lawyer to bring forward a case against industrial pollution in the UK, the first of many such cases, which eventually led to tighter regulations to protect the natural world.

The case, which was pleaded on behalf of the 6th Duke of Buccleuch, was against a paper mill that was pumping industrial waste into the River Esk, which ran through the duke's Dalkeith Estate. Earlier documents show this had been a complaint for decades, but at that time it was a generally accepted practice for mills to pump waste pulp downstream to the detriment of the local ecosystem. Challenging this industrial status quo, Strathern and the duke together successfully pleaded and won the case at the Court of Session, tangentially advancing environmental law. As a result, the natural environment of the Dalkeith Estate was better preserved for future generations.

Nevertheless, Strathern was not the spiritual forebear of

David Attenborough or Greta Thunberg. The case was brought forward at the personal behest of the incumbent duke, and at the time was not regarded by Strathern as a stand for general environmental standards, but the end result was the same.

Strathern also took an early interest in the petrol-guzzling automobiles coming out of Germany and America, becoming so involved that he secured a position as a director of the 'Automobile Engineers and Agents' Rossleigh Ltd, one of the first car dealerships in Britain. Founded in 1890, Rossleigh was formed just five years after the invention of the first mass-produced automobile. Some anecdotal evidence suggests that Strathern did not universally embrace new technologies. Former partner Robert Goudy recounted from his early years at Charlotte Street that Robert Strathern took an intense dislike to the system of voice pipes laced through the office's walls for communication purposes. Instead of speaking into the pipes, the then elderly Strathern would stride out onto a central stairwell and 'loudly and peremptorily' scream out the name of the employee he wanted to see. Despite the bombastic style, this technique was apparently very efficient.

The historical firms saw in the end of the Victorian era and the turn of the century in fair health, each having cultivated reasonably energetic and engaged practices by the standards of the day. It was during this time that Strathern & Blair would represent its first prime minister that we know of, Arthur Balfour, whose family had been represented for at least the previous 150 years. Then, as now, client confidentiality has obscured the details of these partnerships. Nevertheless, prizing open the cast-iron chests revealed something of the life of the last true Victorian partner – at the opposite end of the spectrum to Inglis – Alexander Stevenson Blair.

Inside the sturdiest of the iron chests were found more than 1,500 pages of personal letters to and from Blair. This correspondence predominantly took the form of letter books cataloguing most of his private correspondence from 1888 to 1913. After 1913, it is likely that the chest remained closed for the next 106 years with no interruption: the life and business of a lawyer at the turn of the century, frozen in time. The delicate, tissue-paper-thin pages of the letter books reveal bountiful business advice, society gossip and news from the front at the Boer War.

Alexander Stevenson Blair was quite well known even before the discovery of these items. His presence in the firm was felt long after his death in 1936, continuing through his grandson John Blair and in the stories of the older partners at Strathern & Blair. As late as the 1990s, Alexander Stevenson Blair was remembered as an 'aristocratic figure in his frock-coated morning dress, white spats and gloves and top hat which he wore to the office for many years'. Apparently, this outward appearance was so recognisably ostentatious that once, upon entering a club in Edinburgh with the Duke of Buccleuch, a member exclaimed 'Here comes the Duke of Blair and Mr Buccleuch.' This reputation snowballed throughout his life, as he accumulated several honours including a CBE, the presidency of the Scottish Rugby Union and a position as a member of the king's ceremonial bodyguard in Scotland – established by Sir Walter Scott. This creates a vivid picture of a quintessential Victorian, but the personal letters reveal a more complex figure.

One example found among his letters was his support to women seeking to divorce their husbands – a famously problematic and complex legal challenge at the time. Around the turn of the century, we find extensive detail of Blair's support for a distant acquaintance, Mrs de Falbe, who was seeking a divorce from her husband who had accumulated vast debts and a prodigious record of adultery. The letters, arriving day by day, are a firm expression of his commitment to rid de Falbe of that 'horrible man' and of the vast web of connections he could draw upon across Britain to accomplish the task. For an apparently discounted fee, he provided this service to Mrs de Falbe and several other women at a time when divorce was not only taboo but condemned.

Having fled England, Mrs de Falbe was required to prove both adultery and cruelty. The latter of these was backed by her own personal accounts and those of others, as well as evidence of the sexual diseases her husband had inflicted upon her. Nonetheless, this was not sufficient to prove adultery. To do so, Blair sent letters to contacts across Britain in a call for evidence.

In one, written to 'My Dear Watson', a banker in Inverness, Blair begins 'I want you to do a little detective work for me', as he sends Watson off around Inverness to discover whether Mr de Falbe booked into any hotels with a false 'Mrs de Falbe'. Blair also sets out to find the 'manservant' of Mr de Falbe, who 'as an invaluable mark of identification [has] a large swelling at the lower end of his left cheek, about the size of a pigeon's egg'. Watson responds, having scoured the area, that de Falbe had stayed the night with a woman, recorded as his wife, at the Caledonian Hotel. In the end, they located 'the most damning evidence of his adultery – not once, but on many occasions and at many different places'.

Following a heated exchange of detective work, Blair succeeded in securing the divorce. Along with Watson, he perhaps took inspiration from an esteemed client, Dr Joseph Bell, who was the medical mentor of Arthur Conan Doyle and the acknowledged inspiration for the character of Sherlock Holmes. Or perhaps the inspiration was mutual.

Within his own family, Blair's letters display numerous attempts to hold disparate members together in the face of financial hardship and war. Writing to his nephew Patrick, who was fighting in the Second Boer War, he highlights the situation Patrick's mother finds herself in, being 'in debt to the Butcher to the extent of more than £40 and also to the Baker for another £20'. He also notes that, as a form of security, the baker had taken Patrick's mother's diamond ring. While Blair covered most of the debts of his sister, in search of a more permanent and dignified situation he suggested that Patrick might send some of the money from his lucrative military position to his mother.

Outside the family, several letters show that Blair took it upon himself, from his position of influence, to highlight injustices towards invalided army privates who were unable to work. Writing to the Secretary of State for War, he managed to secure army pensions for several former soldiers who were unable to work due to their injuries. In one case, he mentions the 28-year-old Private Adam Calder, who 'was very severely wounded at the Battle of Magersfontein' leaving him unable to 'undertake any work of a heavy description', and was eking out a living on the streets. Blair's intervention secured Calder the army pension he desperately required, and it seems to have come with the promise of finding the former soldier an appropriate job too. As the Second Boer War was the first major conflict the British had fought in decades, such cases were not in short supply.

The horrors of what was to come later in the twentieth century were made manifest in South Africa, with the cold mechanisation of warfare churning out a bloody harvest. By the end of the Second Boer War, nearly 100,000 British Empire troops were either dead or wounded – by far the most deadly conflict Britain had participated in since the Napoleonic Wars. Nonetheless, the following years saw the UK, and Blair, gradually regain their confidence in Britain's imperial project, albeit with the previous certainty of its destiny shaken. As mentioned earlier, the most recent contents of the chests date from the year before the outbreak of the First World War – a break in time between the old and the new – marking the end of an era of almost unchecked growth and confidence. As the chests were locked shut, the vast and impressive edifice of the legal establishment was about to come crashing down.

A collage of the assorted Writers to Her Majesty's Signet,
imposed over a view of the Signet Library, Edinburgh, c. 1900.

A Collage of Photograph Cut-outs of Writers to the Signet, c. 1900

Standing as a Who's Who of Edinburgh's legal society at the turn of the century, the huge collage on pages 98–99 shows almost every member of HM Society of Writers to the Signet. With individual cut-out photographs of over 300 individuals, it is the ultimate Victorian solution to being unable to organise a group picture. The background to the picture is the Signet Library, the same library that John Davidson helped to bring of age, and for which John Gibson was treasurer during a period of extensive expansion. It is perhaps most notable as the only 'picture' of early partners, with both an Anderson (John Ramsay Anderson) and a Strathern (Robert Strathern) represented, and also includes several other partners such as Alexander Stevenson Blair, Arthur Russell and John Pitman – bringing together several families historically associated with the parent practices. In the top right corner of assembled solicitors, we can also see the marble bust of John Gibson, with his distinctive mutton chops.

6

Solicitors at War: Arthur Russell and Rosemary Mackenzie

'I told her if she was quick she might meet the princess this way, pushed her into the kitchen and turned the key'

Sarajevo, 1914: sparks flew from the barrel of Gavrilo Princip's pistol. Few places were spared from this violent ignition, which eventually reduced to ash the contemporary conception of glorious warfare, and destroyed several million lives. Thousands of miles away, Scots lawyers worked and lived in a world built of mahogany and ornately carved stone, confident in their position, with warfare a heroic sport to be conducted well beyond arms reach. A lifetime without a serious conflict in Europe, and a steady stream of colonial victories spread across the tabloids, gave them and many others cause to believe that the conflict into which they, their families and their businesses would be subsumed might be 'over by Christmas'.

As was the case among most participating nations, almost every man of fighting age was first encouraged, and then conscripted, into the armed forces or supportive industries. Between the historical firms, dozens of men – clerks, secretaries, partners and caretakers – were drafted into the front lines of the First World War. Generally, their social standing decided their military rank: it was regarded as improper for senior civilians to serve under those they employ in peacetime.

Alexander Stevenson Blair perhaps ached more than most for military action and an escape from the office. For several years he had been an officer in the Territorial Army and had a reputation for pomp. Where else could he serve but the 9th Royal Scots, known as the 'Dandy Ninth' for their glamorous Highland dress, and by then part of the oldest extant regiment in the British Army. Being composed of fighting-age men from Edinburgh and its environs, the regiment had an eclectic social mix with a high proportion of lawyers, rugby players and artists as well as dock workers and labourers. Blair, who was eventually given the rank of Lieutenant Colonel, was mobilised within the 9th Royal Scots at the outbreak of war. During the first few months they trained and waited in Britain, only being deployed to France in February of 1915 by which point the British Army had already dug in, waiting for the other side to act.

In France, Blair and the battalion faced immediate frontline action. In what came to be known as their 'baptism of fire', the 9th participated, under the command of Blair, in the second and third Battles of Ypres, at Vimy Ridge and, perhaps most devastatingly, in the months-long Battle of the Somme. At some point, near Fontaine-lès-Cappy, the 9th were entrenched in a heavily mined area, with several soldiers sustaining signs of shell shock. One of them, Second Lieutenant Arthur Annandale, was so shaken by one explosion he took an opportunity to flee the trenches, only to be captured. The penalty for desertion was death. Blair intervened in the subsequent court martial, providing a positive character statement for the officer and, crucially, supporting the position that he was suffering from neurasthenia. In the end, Annandale avoided death.

Heading up a nexus of communications on the western front, Blair produced field reports that reveal surprising wartime operations. For example, in the now declassified reports, we are told of the arrival of 'No. 15 Mobile Laboratory' – a new piece of military technology intended to detect outbreaks of typhoid and other diseases in the trenches, with the aim of preserving manpower. The reports also document the arrival of soldiers from India and other parts of the British Empire, with several thousand passing through in just a few days in October 1917. A sixth of all British Empire troops were from India, so this would not have been an unusual sight. Nevertheless, not all the soldiers drafted in from the Empire were willing combatants. While Blair was the Commandant of communications in the Abancourt area, a mutinous New Zealander, Private John Braithwaite, was court martialled and, to make an example of him, shot for treason. For various reasons, from death in action to disease or execution, of the 6,000 men to pass through the ranks of the Dandy Ninth, more than 1,000 would never return. Among them was Alexander Stevenson Blair's eldest son, Patrick.

A permanent reminder of this era was found alongside the chests in the current office of Anderson Strathern at Rutland Court. At the end of the war, Strathern & Blair commissioned a wooden memorial to all those company employees who had died during the war: Captain J. MacKay, Lieutenant P. MacPhail, Lieutenant J. Stewart, Lieutenant W. Woodrow, Sergeant H. Reid, Private W. Redpath and Private W. Smith. For a law firm operating out of a single building, with just a couple of partners and a small staff, this toll was considerable. To put the rate in perspective, if replicated in the firm today, the total death toll would have been almost a hundred.

As a generation of men were sent off to the front, with many not to return, positions that had always been occupied by men were temporarily filled by women. As the war wore on and protections against conscription for those performing legal clerical work were rescinded, government campaigns were launched to bring women into the office. Women had always been a part of legal life – with the wives and daughters of lawyers such as

War Memorial, Strathern & Blair, c. 1919

This simple wooden memorial is inscribed with the names of seven men who were killed in action during the First World War. These men were non-partner solicitors, clerks and apprentices, all but two serving in officer roles. The death toll among officers was especially high, perhaps as much as 20%, with the death rate for soldiers overall around 10%.

In a timely coincidence, this memorial was rediscovered on 10 November 2018, the 100th anniversary of the last full day of fighting in the First World War. Though it is the only war memorial which survives of the historical practices, it is not a comprehensive list of all those associated with the firm who died in the First World War. If the Second World War is also included, it is likely that all historical practices associated with the modern-day firm together suffered around 20–30 fatalities. Many have their names inscribed on stone tablets in the Signet Library.

A war memorial of the firm that was rediscovered almost exactly 100 years after the 1918 armistice.

Alexander Duncan at times taking complete control of the business temporarily. Women had also started to work as typists in some businesses, although the generally conservative spaces of the legal profession were among the last places for women to formally take up posts.

Nevertheless, the lack of male substitutes, and unsustainable overreliance on elderly men to pick up the work, allowed women to breach this important male industry for the first time. By 1917 the Ministry of National Service was recruiting over 5,000 women per week to free up men from clerical positions, and from this pool came the first women to work formally in a clerical role at the New Town law firms. Women proved themselves just as capable as their male counterparts.

As women met the challenge of taking on the work of their male predecessors this brought about a change in attitudes in British society. Perhaps this shift in perception is best expressed in the way male propagandists portrayed the role of women throughout the conflict. At the outbreak of war, one poster encouraged women to support male relatives to take up the call to arms. The poster is captioned 'Women of Britain say Go!' and features elegant women forlornly gazing through a window, clutching one another as a child tugs on their flowing dresses. At the war's end, propagandists were instead encouraging women to take up work that included heavy industry and agriculture. A poster of this era is proudly emblazoned with 'On Her Their Lives Depend – Enrol at Once!', speaking directly to women. In it, a female munitions worker confidently looks forward, decked out in factory uniform, behind her the heavy artillery she has assembled. Nevertheless, while ingrained prejudices of the capabilities of British women had been eroded over the course of the war, women still faced an uphill battle for equal opportunity.

Factories and fields were one thing – women had always made up a large part of the industrial and rural workforce – the law was another. Although women had now entered the office in clerical roles, hotly defended and often absurd reasons were peddled to prevent them from practising as solicitors. Among the favourites was the 'observation' of the legal scholar Glenville, who claimed that it was a physically impractical placement as a woman's voice could not carry as far as a man's in a courtroom, and that, in order to uphold chivalry, men would be forced to give in to a woman's arguments. Even more bizarre was a popular belief that women would use their 'wiles' in court to overpower their opponent.

Outdated pseudoscience born from the creepy world of Victorian eugenics was also wheeled out to insist that the female brain lacked the logical capacity to work through arguments in the same way as the male brain, and that the emotional impact of the case would prove debilitating and bring on frequent spells of fainting. In reality, this was just another case of a comfortable elite seeking to see off the new meritocracy, fearing that by rocking the boat they themselves might go overboard. It would also be wrong to suggest that women were accepted into the workplace elsewhere in the pecking order: one account shows that a clerk at J&F Anderson tried to stop women from entering the firm because of the lack of designated toilet facilities.

As the war finally came to an end, the liberties the government had promised required consolidation in both law and culture. There was a backlash against the rise of women from the older generation of solicitors, including Robert Strathern. This was not a universal attitude. Following years in the trenches, many of the younger solicitors and clerks were enthused by the new change in approach, albeit one where women were still firmly prevented from securing the top jobs.

Attempts at returning to the past were further set back when Scotland admitted Madge Easton Anderson to the legal profession in 1920. Anderson was the first female lawyer anywhere in the UK, and required an Act of Parliament to allow her admittance. Further obstacles were put in her path, as the Scottish

Law Agents Society regarded her apprenticeship as void because it had begun before the Act of Parliament permitting women to practise law was passed. In what might be regarded as her first successful case, Anderson took the society to the Court of Session, where it was concluded that her petition to become a law agent should be granted. Following a successful early career in her native Glasgow, she went on to establish the first legal firm run by a woman anywhere in the UK in 1931.

Arthur Russell was one of the cadre of male lawyers who embraced the admittance of women to the law. Having entered the law in the 1890s, he went against the tide of the older generation, but having fought in the trenches as a captain in the Argyll and Sutherland Highlanders he had earned the respect of his colleagues in this conviction.

For years before, Russell had been known as an unconventional and energetic character, finding close companions among both men and women in his explorations and documentation of the natural world. Russell, equipped with an early tripod camera and journal, was possibly the first in the world to document in photographic detail the Munros of Scotland with the assistance of his band of mountaineers. It was a passion that would dominate his life, his career at Strathern & Blair and his legacy as a founder of the National Trust for Scotland.

Russell's desire to explore was insatiable. From his collection of travel diaries, now held at the National Museum of Scotland, we gain something of a picture of this pursuit and its consequences, as well as the efforts expended to break from the constrictive work schedules of a Victorian law firm. In 1895, when Russell was still a young man, he writes of his trip, tripod camera in tow, to the tallest of the four Munros of the Cairngorms, carried out at breakneck speed:

> The short climb of Good Friday made me turn my way again to the Cairngorms especially as the weather

was very settled, clear and bright with a moderate east wind, so being fortunate to get Alec Fraser we left on Wednesday night at 9.30pm for Perth, carriage to ourselves, good game of chess, I lost but should have made it a draw. At Perth Station we put in fully 1½ miles on the platform ere we left at 12.40am, the guard getting us a carriage to ourselves. It was a fine night, from about Struan the view back over Ben y Vrackie very fine in the yellow light; up by Dalwhinnie the white clouds were quite low, slept very little; Aviemore at 3.50am, went to Waiting Room and soon had cocoa ready and having arranged rucksacks etc. left by 4.35am; the sun just scattering the clouds on Cairngorm. A steady swing brought us up past near Coylum Bridge and on to near the Bothy in Einich at 6.40am where we halted for breakfast of brown bread and Melton Mowbray pie. Even the lower slopes of Braeriach were scarcely visible owing to the heavy cloud still hanging over the hill and all up Glen Einich. By 7.10am we were away.

Over the next day, Russell and Fraser climbed four of the 4,000ft hills – stopping for chess, cocoa and the chance to photograph the soaring peaks and deep glens with their rudimentary but sturdy camera. Eventually, at 7.30pm, they made their descent from the sunny peaks back to the station, with Russell recording that they had covered 35 miles in their 17½ hours of climbing, including the walks to and from the station. The two made it back to Edinburgh's Haymarket station just after 8am, allowing Russell an hour to catch his breath before making it to the office before 10am. He noted afterwards that he 'Felt sleepy during afternoon but that was all. Several days till my face recovered, the whole skin nearly peeling off with the sun.'

As the years went on, the friendships garnered from such trips earned him a new client, the Association for the Protection of Rural Scotland. The reach of this organisation was limited, as it lacked the resources of the new National Trust in England. Protection alone for these areas was not enough, preservation and acquisition had to be the objective, for natural as well as historical treasures. With this aim, in 1931 Arthur Russell and several others formed the National Trust for Scotland (NTS). In the new organisation, which became a client of Strathern & Blair, Russell served as solicitor, treasurer and secretary. He was what his friend the Labour MP Tam Dalyell called 'the dynamic driving force behind the creation of the Trust'.

In the beginning, Russell and the NTS were equipped with little more than charm, luck and a reliance on the generosity of others. A fortuitous acquisition took place in 1935 when Russell and his son George headed to a land auction, seeking to secure the Signal Rock at Glencoe. This prominent outcrop was supposedly the point where, in 1692, the secretly pro-government Campbell chief gave the signal to massacre their hosts, the Jacobite MacDonalds, in one of the most notorious betrayals in Scottish history.

The NTS had mustered £1,500 to buy the unnecessarily large site, which included the rock, but a serendipitous turn of events delivered it into their laps, free of charge. The night before the auction, the two men, who were camping at the auction site, made their way to the local pub and by chance sat beside a rival bidder for the huge tract of land, Alister Sutherland. The men apparently got along to such an extent that Sutherland promised to gift the Signal Rock to the Trust should he win the auction – which he did the following day. With £1,500 going spare, the Russells wasted no time in turning their attention to the acquisition of the Aonach Eagach ridge, one of the most dramatic mountain landscapes in Britain. This acquisition was especially pertinent to Arthur Russell, as he was the first person to traverse its perilous ridge from west to east over 30 years earlier.

In later years, Russell was also a strong proponent of the Country House Scheme whereby families could pass ownership of stately homes to the Trust while still living in them. Today, we might wrongly assume that these stately homes and castles, not to mention their grounds, have always been regarded as worthy of preservation – but at that time they were often regarded as archaic and unfashionable, not to mention economically unviable, and as a result many such buildings were simply demolished. This was the fate of almost all of the estates of the East India Company merchants who had returned to Britain, as well as the estates of Alexander Duncan and John Davidson. Scotland's history, warts and all, was slowly being dissolved, abolished in a wave of arrogant disdain.

Arthur Russell's son George – who became a partner at Charlotte Street in 1936 – was among the most fearsome opponents of this destruction. In large part, his opposition took the form of persuading stately home owners to gift their properties to the Trust, and encouraging visiting dignitaries to back the Trust's conservation work. He was helped in this task by the fact that, as chauffeur to the Trust's chairmen, he travelled to North America, where he encouraged people to visit Scotland following the boom of transatlantic aviation. George gradually took on the Trust's legal work as his father approached retirement. But before some of Scotland's historic properties could be handed over to the NTS, they would have to serve as barracks, intelligence stations and hospitals. Grim news was sounding out across the wireless sets of Castle Street, Charlotte Street and the country.

As was the case with millions of other men and women across Britain, George Russell signed up almost immediately for service in what would become the Second World War. Left behind were the partners and employees who had fought in the previous conflict, too old for the front but still needed for the effort at home. Along with business partner Arthur Blair, Russell found himself confined to the mainland at the start of the war, eventually being attached to the Polish Armoured Division, which was based in Scotland after being forced to retreat from its homeland. When the time came, Russell crossed the Channel as part of the Allied invasion of Normandy, helping to establish the Polish Headquarters in Normandy and later Belgium. For his efforts, he was appointed OBE, awarded the Polish Golden Cross of Merit with Swords and inducted into the Belgian Ordre de la Couronne. George went on to act for the National Trust for Scotland for a further 30 years, later passing the mantle to his own son who, in 2019, followed in his grandfather's steps in an expedition across the Aonach Eagach ridge.

At Castle Street, partner Ian Pitman was among many to enlist in 1939. Following months of waiting in northern France with no sign of German advance, Pitman was captured in 1940 at St Valery as he helped cover the retreat of the bulk of the British Army to Dunkirk. For the next five years, he would be engaged in what he described as a 'long sojourn in Poland and elsewhere', only being released at the end of the war. Although being a prisoner of war was a miserable and uncertain experience, Pitman survived his confinement and even befriended the conservationist and ornithologist George Waterston in the prisoner-of-war camp Oflag 7c. Pitman discovered that Waterston owned Fair Isle, a hot spot for bird migrations in the North Sea.

When the war finally ended, on the return voyage to Scotland from Poland, their ship took them via the Northern Isles passing Fair Isle, which even from a distance was teeming with life. As Pitman and Waterston watched the seabirds from the ship deck they conceived the idea of establishing a major bird observatory on Fair Isle. With the help of Pitman, Waterston realised this vision almost immediately upon his return to Scotland, and would later gift the island, through J&F Anderson, to the National Trust for Scotland. Despite the distress and bravery involved in both of these wartime journeys, they appear fortunate compared with that of the youngest partner the law firm ever had.

Ian Drummond Mackenzie was only in his mid twenties when he became a partner at Charlotte Street. He was the son of a professor of chemistry and later studied modern languages, but seems to have reluctantly taken up a career in the law. He was described by others as a gentle and generous young man, and shy for someone of his profession. At the outbreak of the Second World War, Mackenzie enlisted with the Seaforth Highlanders, although he found himself grounded in Britain for the early months of the war as the two sides waited for the other to blink. The blink, when it came, was blitzkrieg and resulted in the fall of most of Western Europe and the evacuation of the entire British army in the space of a few weeks. However, Mackenzie was not caught up in the evacuations of Dunkirk; he was being trained in reconnaissance in preparation for covert operations in Britain's far-flung colonial possessions.

Before being posted abroad, Mackenzie married Rosemary Munro at St Cuthbert's Church in Edinburgh. Rosemary and Ian had met at Strathern & Blair, where Rosemary worked as a secretary and was known for her sharp humour. Around the advent of war, she had worked as a replacement secretary to the Duke of Buccleuch, drafting letters to 'Loopy' on behalf of the duke; only later did she discover that Loopy was King Leopold III of Belgium. Later in life, Rosemary recounted how she had fallen in love with Ian Mackenzie, engaging with his true passions beyond the law, while helping him to find fulfilment in the career ahead of him. In the end, they had less than a month together before Ian was shipped off to Cherbourg and the Middle East, by then the most active zone of conflict in the war.

Given events in Europe, the defensive task for Ian Mackenzie and the rest of the Eighth Army – to prevent the advancing German forces from taking Egypt, the Suez Canal and the wider Middle East – was difficult to carry out. This was primarily to secure the huge supplies of oil and raw materials in the region, as well as maintain Suez as a fast route to India, which provided vital resources to the forces in Europe. If Suez was lost, the Allied war machine would grind to a halt, necessitating a near-total capitulation to the Axis powers of Germany, Italy and Japan. This crucial objective was coupled with the challenge of facing off an as-yet-unbeaten adversary, the highly capable General Rommel, who in 1942 had begun to advance towards the Suez Canal. In contrast to the German forces, still drunk on victory, the Allied forces in the region were exhausted.

The Second Battle of El Alamein in November of 1942 had to be decisive should the Eighth Army have any hope of turning the tide of war. Before the battle began, Mackenzie was tasked with securing information on the enemy, putting himself at considerable risk of harm. It is unclear what form this investigation took, though we do know Mackenzie was involved in close observation of enemy forces. The intelligence Mackenzie and others gathered proved to be surprisingly decisive in the eventual strategy of the Allied commanders, as it confirmed the Axis forces were fewer than previously thought, and only had two days' worth of reserve supplies. The flow of supplies was discovered to be reliant on two small and vulnerable ports, with lines already overstretched. With the prospect of being starved out, Rommel decided to go on the offensive. The fighting continued for several days, and eventually the Axis army was forced into retreat, the first significant British victory in the war. Rommel and his forces retreated to Tunisia, and eventually to Italy.

In the wake of this much-needed reprieve, and in the process of cleaning up the last pockets of Axis forces before an invasion of Italy, Mackenzie was tasked with leading reconnaissance missions in the still-occupied Djerba region of Tunisia. While completing this mission, Mackenzie was killed by enemy fire, one of the last fatalities of the North Africa campaign. He was buried along with more than a thousand other soldiers at the nearby Sfax Commonwealth Cemetery.

Upon receiving news of her husband's death, rather than languish in grief, Rosemary almost immediately packed her bags and volunteered to work overseas with the Young Women's Christian Organisation (YWCA). Leaving behind her life in Edinburgh, she set off for Stranraer where women were trained to nurse injured troops. While at these training grounds, Rosemary was selected along with some other young women for an audience with Princess Mary, who was touring the training camps. She later recounted, 'just before the princess arrived, a formidable lady came up to me and said, "who are you?" I told her and said we were waiting to be presented. She said, "you are far too young", and proceeded to tell me why she should be in the line. I told her if she was quick she might meet the princess this way, pushed her into the kitchen and turned the key in the door.'

When Rosemary was eventually despatched she was responsible for caring for furloughed soldiers at Bari in southern Italy. Bari, like most of Italy apart from Mussolini's rump state in the north, had switched sides by this stage as the invasion of Italy got underway, but it was no safe haven. In December 1943, the Luftwaffe bombed the city and its harbour, killing more than a thousand and sinking seventeen ships. This air raid also led to a further unintentional, and deadly, consequence. There were secret supplies of mustard gas, intended for use by the Allies if the Germans resorted to chemical warfare, in storage aboard the ships. When the ships were destroyed, the poisonous gas fumes spread over the city, with many fatalities – although the cause of the deaths was covered up until decades later. Bari gained the unwelcome distinction of being the only European city to suffer from a chemical attack in the Second World War.

In 1945, when Rosemary was working as a welfare officer, the city suffered a further disaster when the US Navy ship the ss *Charles Henderson*, carrying 2,000 tons of aerial bombs, exploded in the harbour, leading to 360 deaths and nearly 2,000 wounded. Rosemary would have probably been on hand as a YWCA nurse for both disasters. With her late husband's regiment one of many that travelled from northern Africa to the south of Italy, Rosemary made it her mission to tend the injured soldiers who had fought alongside Ian.

Rosemary Mackenzie survived the war and returned to Scotland soon after it ended. She found a changed country in which many people, men and women alike, were determined not to repeat the mistakes of the past. Many were reluctant to pick up where they had left off. Rosemary was among them, choosing to move on from her secretarial role at the firm. Given that she and her late husband had met in the office, returning there might have carried painful memories. Instead, Rosemary returned to her Highland hometown, Tain. Here, she established herself as a historian and in 1966 founded a museum to celebrate 900 years of Tain's history. Rosemary was made an MBE and visited by members of the royal family, most prominently the Queen Mother, who often stayed in the nearby Castle of Mey. The museum that Rosemary founded still operates in Tain.

For women, the war had broken down traditional barriers and opened up new positions in the workplace. In some ways, this advancement built on the foundations laid by the First World War, which had already established women in secretarial and administrative roles. The Second World War enabled women to advance further, with many more becoming lawyers in their own right in the years after the war. The first woman to break through to a position of formal authority among the historical firms was Margaret Maud Mitchell, the only female partner of J&F Anderson. She was enrolled as a law agent on 6 July 1940 – at 27 years old – just a few weeks after the fall of France and the Dunkirk evacuations. Entering 48 Castle Street for the first time as a fully qualified solicitor, she might have heard updates on the unfolding Battle of Britain over the wireless. At any rate, it inspired her to sign up for the Women's Auxiliary Air Force from 1942 to 1946.

Edith Latto was another secretary at J&F Anderson who took on legal work when male solicitors were called to the front. In this capacity, she worked as part-secretary, part-solicitor under Pat Smyth, who had fought in the First World War and was left with sole responsibility for the firm throughout the Second World War. A son of the manse, Pat was in his fifties when the war broke out. His son had enlisted in the RAF, notorious for its high mortality rate, adding further pressure on the partner.

Threats to the lives and livelihoods of Edith, Margaret and Pat were always on the horizon. Through the early part of the war, the Luftwaffe targeted the docks at Leith and Granton, as well as civilian areas, in a strategy intended to induce terror and surrender. Despite the considerable risk taken in not seeking shelter in such a raid, night after night, Pat Smyth and Edith Latto stood guard over the Castle Street offices on the lookout for incendiary bombs. Although such a bomb never hit the offices or any near it, they were determined to save as much as possible before the fire could spread. Given that the building was bursting at the seams with 250 years of paperwork, the fire would not have lacked kindling.

7

A Lawful Union

'If Pat fell ill while Ena was on holiday we'd be up a gum tree'

When the war was over, every village, town and city erupted into hysterical celebrations. Douglas Stewart, an apprentice of Strathern & Blair and later partner at J&F Anderson, was in central Edinburgh on VE day. He recounted the extreme elation and release as, before a crowd of thousands, the city's lights, which had been blacked out and extinguished for several years, finally leapt back to life. Just two weeks away from his eighteenth birthday, Stewart celebrated with friends across the city, eventually ending up at the French consulate where they celebrated with their Gallic comrades till dawn.

It would be months or longer after VE day before troops and prisoners of war finally made it back to Britain. It was only then that the strain felt by partners and clerks such as Pat Smyth and Edith Latto was alleviated, although some of those who fought in the war did not wish to return to the law.

Britain was filled with renewed confidence and vigour, striving to eliminate the Beveridge Report's five giants, 'Want, Disease, Ignorance, Squalor and Idleness'. Nowhere would be entirely immune from the subsequent restructuring of society, least of all the oak-panelled offices of Scottish lawyers. Inheriting fundamentally Victorian practices originally built around one or two partners, with the heavy lifting done by a handful of clerks and apprentices, the firms were about to become spread much thinner, with expertise moving from the generalist to the specialist. It is therefore more difficult to single out certain individuals as representative of an era. These were gradual changes, spanning decades, and rarely linear. The story of the past 75 years is that of specialisation and diversification, powered by a punishing level of competition from which only a small number of firms would emerge, changed.

Many of the pioneers of this new world were women. Soon after the war, Edith Latto retrained as a qualified lawyer, allowing her to become an 'associate' of J&F Anderson along with Margaret Maud Mitchell, who was acting as a de facto partner. It would only be after Latto's departure, and over two decades of service as a qualified solicitor, that Mitchell would be awarded full partner status in the 1960s, becoming one of the very first female partners in any of Scotland's law firms. Strathern & Blair did not appoint its first female partners, Fiona Gibb and Lynda Pennell, until 1988. Nevertheless, Gibb and Pennell were the first female partners among any of the prestigious law firms based at Charlotte Square, demonstrating just how recently fundamental first steps were being taken.

As the practices expanded, the workforces did too, with a need for new roles and responsibilities. Throughout the 1950s and 1960s, Strathern & Blair employed a couple, the Chapmans, as the caretakers of 12 Charlotte Street, where they lived in the ground-floor flat. The cockney Sergeant Chapman met his future wife while stationed in India during the Second World War, after which they came back to Britain and married. Together, they helped maintain the now ageing premises, with Sergeant Chapman greeting clients upon arrival and leading them to the appropriate solicitor. When he began working for the firm in the early 1950s, the rapid stream of titled clients passing through the office every day caused him to remark 'Working here ain't like working in a law office, it's like working in the House of Lords!' He was not far off in this judgement, with several peers, including the Earls of Bute, the Dukes of Buccleuch and Alec Douglas-Home (who renounced his peerage upon becoming prime minister) being clients at this time.

Castle Street also had caretakers, who lived in the large apartment on the top floor of the building: George and Betty Northey ran the office from 1963 through to 1989. This tradition is continued today by their granddaughter, Georgie Northey, who manages the reception at Rutland Court, having grown up in the apartments above J&F Anderson. She remembers the old building with nostalgia, recalling helping out by licking stamps in the mail room, inspecting the suits of armour in the boardroom, as well as sneaking to the staff coffee machine after hours to buy hot chocolate for 5p. In recalling her childhood at Castle Street, Georgie also remembered being shown a ring which, the story has it, once belonged to Bonnie Prince Charlie. Given the range of strange items that have emerged from the investigation of the Nuremberg chests, it is possible such an object was in the firm's possession at that time.

At another of the company's historical practices, Bell & Scott, Bruce & Kerr WS (the merged successor to Alexander Duncan's practice Bruce & Kerr WS), the guard was also changing. Alan Masson, taken on as an apprentice in 1976, was one of the first openly gay solicitors in Scotland. At that time, to admit to being what criminal law referred to as a 'self-confessed homosexual' was seen as career suicide. However, after qualifying, Masson was kept on and in 1980 was sent on secondment to J&F Anderson to acquire experience in litigation. In 1981 he returned to Bell & Scott, Bruce & Kerr WS, was admitted as a Writer to the Signet and a few months later became a partner in the firm at the age of 29.

The fact that Masson was made a partner in 1981 is all the more remarkable given that, in Scotland, homosexuality was illegal until 1980 (compared with 1967 in England and

Wales). As one of the first openly gay partners in any Scottish law firm, he also entered a social environment tailored for the male solicitor and his wife. This was epitomised by the 'Partners and Wives' dinner: after the arrival of Masson and his future husband Richard, this was quietly renamed the 'Partners and Partners' dinner.

Masson recounted that the working environment was welcoming and relaxed, and being gay was never a problem for him within the firm. Nor was it many years later when, having in the interim left (the by now) Bell & Scott WS to specialise as an employment lawyer, he came full circle and joined Anderson Strathern in 2006 as a partner in the firm. He was later elected to the board, became the firm's IT partner and spent the final years of his legal career as the firm's Chief Operating Officer.

Despite some typically Victorian prejudices and prohibitions being gradually eroded, the physical office environment of the 1970s remained much as it had a century before. The interior of the buildings was relatively unchanged since their construction in the eighteenth and nineteenth centuries: twisting warrens of corridors connecting individual offices broken up only by dark stairwells and the occasional meeting room – a far cry from the open-plan offices of the early twenty-first century. The set-up was intensely hierarchal with ferocious competition for the most highly sought-after spaces. This established order was dismantled not only by a growing desire for greater connectivity, but also by the hunt for the new big beasts of officedom – the photocopier, the word processor, the central computer, the fax machine.

In the early days, computers were generally regarded, and mocked, as more at home in NASA's Apollo Space Programme than in an old Scottish law firm. In the 1960s, they took up whole rooms in exchange for not very much – making them only practical for the most advanced mathematical endeavours.

By the late 1970s, however, the technology was becoming more affordable, more compact and more useful, with real-world application for businesses dealing in large quantities of data. To many, computers were fascinating and frustrating in equal measure and, accompanied by the prophecy that embracing new technology would make or break professions across the board, just a bit frightening. Many in the legal world were reluctant to take on these ferociously expensive and complicated machines, which threatened to change working practices at every level.

As with other small, historical firms, J&F Anderson was eventually forced to confront the new reality head-on. In the transcript of a 1982 partnership meeting, the fatal flaw with the human-based knowledge storage system was spelled out in black and white: 'If Pat fell ill while Ena was on holiday we'd be up a gum tree.' Many a sleepless night was probably spent dwelling on this doomsday scenario. And there may have been more brooding on the expense of the remedy. In the same document we discover a central computer system would cost £40,000 – which with payments spread out and including maintenance would be £15,000 per annum – and each word processor would cost a further £10,000. Compared to the typical salary of typists and secretaries this was a considerable expense, which only paid off in the long term. But the immediate benefits of a central catalogue of information that was easy to edit and replicate were required to keep pace with larger competitors. As is common with automation, the arrival came with a human cost: several individuals who had devoted decades to the firm found their functions increasingly obsolete. This included Henry Nevan, a highly respected older member of J&F Anderson, who had started as an errand boy at 14 and had worked up to head cashier, a de facto partner, over the following 60 years. In the end, all the historical practices signed up to the exorbitant price of modernisation, but largely avoided a Faustian pact of staying afloat at the expense of their corporate souls. Older members of the firms who had previously been responsible for work now carried out by computers were retained with new responsibilities.

A hand-drawn data input card from the minutes of
a board meeting of J&F Anderson, visualising the first
stages of computerisation (1983).

When the computers eventually arrived at J&F Anderson in 1984 they appear to have been treated with caution. Comfortingly familiar libraries and overfilled record rooms were ditched to house the huge machines: a sign of progress for some, a sign of doom for others. The subsequent partnership meetings record the challenge of wrestling with this new, unknown entity, slowly learning how best to utilise its systems and tend to its needs. The first point of action was setting a password. They eventually settled on 123 and, as a back-up, ABC – it would be several years before technological advances would allow for this to be changed to 'password'. At first the firm neglected to switch the new machines off at night or over the weekend, causing them to continually overheat and crash.

Eventually, personal computers, as well as a central main-frame, were brought into the respective offices, considerably reducing the time spent endlessly leafing through old documents in search of a note or precedent. Hand-typed documents became a thing of the past, though this computerisation proved a double-edged sword for any hoping for simpler, easier work. The new-found accessibility of vast supplies of information resulted in considerably more reading and research than previously expected, and the ease at which documents could be written and edited led to much longer, not shorter, reports and facsimiles. As soon as people got the hang of the new systems, they were outdated, and with the need to keep pace, an even newer system had to be bought and integrated. The whole process was costly but effective, and ultimately essential. It is also one common to most historical businesses surviving today: those who failed to adapt did not survive.

The technological advances enabled increasingly complex work to be carried out, and diversification beyond landed and private clients. At J&F Anderson, this included the Crown Estate, a huge public body that manages rural, coastal and marine assets of the Crown. It was Douglas Stewart, the apprentice at Strathern & Blair, who brought this client into the fold after he was made a partner in 1961. Although outwardly the Crown Estates work appeared similar to that of traditional landed clients, it would soon take the firm into uncharted waters. Oil had been found in the North Sea, and this was incredibly pertinent to the Crown Estate, not only because the considerable infrastructure would have to pass through several properties and coastal areas, but also because some of the oilfields lay within the maritime jurisdiction of the Crown, entitling them to a portion of revenues. Stewart flew from Edinburgh to Shetland on a regular basis to ensure the smooth implementation of drilling contracts and infra-structure projects, and recalls that, flying over the east coast of Scotland, there was hardly a break in the trenches being dug for pipelines to be laid between the several entrepôts and the refinery at Grangemouth. In this work, Stewart also often had to negotiate directly with lawyers in the small towns along Scotland's north-east coast whom he regarded as being of excellent quality, giving the legal professionals of Edinburgh and Glasgow a run for their money. Oil proved to be a shot in the arm to the ailing Scottish economy.

By the mid 1980s both J&F Anderson and Strathern & Blair were two very-long-established, reputable, medium-sized practices with a strong client base. They had both weathered the move from the Victorian-style workplace with relative success, a move which had gone hand-in-hand with a move away from their exclusive recruitment of privately educated men. For both businesses, this ended the reliance on the personal wealth of partners to guarantee security, and instead demanded a more rapid and reliable turnover based upon the work of a much greater number of specialised partners. Meetings of the full partnership, which had ballooned from a few individuals to over a dozen, became rarer. Instead, specialisation into financial, commercial, private client and policy work committees became necessary. Coupled with this, the feudal framework for land ownership and transaction in Scotland was now almost completely dismantled, cutting off a long-held area of expertise. Nevertheless, this fading era still held sway at the end of the century, symbolised for J&F Anderson in the granting of a coat of arms by the Lord Lyon in 1990. It was accompanied by a motto in Latin, *A posse ad esse*, 'If it is possible it will be done.'

Such a metamorphosis could have sounded the death knell of practices with roots sunk deep into Scotland's past, and for many it did, but the change encouraged J&F Anderson and Strathern & Blair to be more proactive in finding routes to improve and expand their businesses. In 1974 J&F Anderson took on an office in Haddington that specialised in property sales. Strathern & Blair managed to find considerable private-client work with overseas investors looking to expand into Scotland. With heightened expectations for lawyers to have a full university education, the old, and largely disliked, practice of concurrent study at university with apprenticeship was scrapped in favour of a full university degree followed by a traineeship.

---

14 Court Street, Haddington (Anderson Strathern)

In 1974 McVies WS, based in the centre of Haddington, was acquired by J&F Anderson. The smallest of Anderson Strathern's offices, 14 Court Street primarily focuses on property law and caters for a number of local and national clients. Since it became a part of the firm, it has been delivering a service to rural clients in the east of Scotland. As the birthplace of John Davidson, one of the founders of the modern-day firm, Haddington holds a significant place in the firm's story.

The disparate, and somewhat tangled, strands of Anderson Strathern's history finally interweave as the senior partners of J&F Anderson and Strathern & Blair, Nigel Buchanan and John Blair respectively, met to discuss the merger of the two practices. There were two main reasons for the necessity of joining the practices: one new, one old. The strain to remain technologically innovative, with continual investment in computer systems that quickly became obsolete, was a novel challenge. The other issue had been rumbling around in plain sight since the time of John Davidson, though was only now coming to maturity. It is even printed in the foundational book that Davidson contributed research towards, *The Wealth of Nations*, where Adam Smith explains the problem in his famous analogy of the manufacture of a pin.

In considering the production of a single pin, Smith first discusses the output of a blacksmith who completes all the necessary tasks in the production of a single pin, with an expert capable of producing about 700 pins a day. Then Smith considers a system whereby:

> One . . . draws out the wire; another straights it; a third cuts it; a fourth points it; a fifth grinds it at the top for receiving the head; to make the head requires two or three distinct operations; to put it on is a peculiar business; to whiten the pins is another; it is even a trade by itself to put them into the paper; and the important business of making a pin is, in this manner, divided into about eighteen distinct operations.

This method produces upwards of 4,800 pins per person per day. The same principle might be applied to a law firm. To achieve the holistic and quality service necessary to meet the increasingly complex requirements of clients, traditional firms with a wide client base had to scale up and become collections of interconnected specialists. The generalist was dead, long live the specialist.

Scale and specialisation therefore went hand in hand with quality and reliability, and it was on these principles that the merger was agreed. However, as preparations were underway for a huge transfer of staff between the two offices and a rationalisation of departments, it was agreed that effectiveness should not come at the cost of the ethos of the practices. To preserve the independent stories of both firms, the firms employed someone to write a short booklet *A Lawful Union*. The brief was reasonably straightforward, albeit with a somewhat unambitious expectation: 'I am afraid it has to be somewhat dry.' To complete the task of recounting such a sprawling history, the researcher drew on the huge stores of documentation held at both firms at the time, as well as the '162 trunks and 23 sacks' left at the NRS. In the end, it preserved the oral histories at that time, and shed a light on the distant past, strengthening the decision to bind the firms together. When the firms merged on 1 September 1992 to become Anderson Strathern they did not become something new, but rather represented a continuation of something very old.

The divergent branches finally came together with the merger of Bell & Scott, the successor to Alexander Duncan's historical practice, with Anderson Strathern in 2011. They brought with them a host of historical clients, some of which had been with them since the time of Duncan. A few years before the merger, they ran into treacherous waters while acting for one client – the Bible Board of Scotland – an organisation set up by Queen Victoria to authorise the printing of the King James Bible in Scotland. Since that establishment, a member of Bell & Scott had served as clerk to the board, and in 1998 Andrew Kerr, the senior partner, was serving as clerk when the board incurred the wrath of religious fundamentalists across the globe. The Bible Board had just approved among the most controversial publications of scripture that century.

The proposal of the prospective publisher, Canongate Books, was seemingly simple – to offer individual books of the King James Bible as 'Pocket Canons', each book beginning with a modern introduction by a well-known author. The serious issue lay in the content of the introductions. The publisher had chosen a diverse range of authors, including the Dalai Lama, Will Self and Nick Cave, some of whom used phrases that did not go down well with certain groups. For example, the Book of Revelation was described as 'a guignol of tedium, a portentous horror film', another writer referred to Jesus as 'self-assured, pushy and somewhat dislikable' and another described the Old Testament God as 'a mad, bloodthirsty and capricious despot' easily mistaken for the Devil himself. The deluge of criticism was of biblical proportions.

Although the publications won praise among liberal Christians and secular commentators, not a single Christian bookseller in Britain would stock the book. Furthermore, John Shearer, of the United Protestant Council, decried the publications as 'the worst bit of blasphemous libel we have ever seen in this country' and encouraged Christians everywhere to take action. In contrast, Richard Holloway, the Bishop of Edinburgh and only churchman to contribute to the publications, dismissed the claims of blasphemy, saying, 'This reaction comes from a particularly narrow religious background and doesn't acknowledge that the Bible is a library of books which can be read in all sorts of ways.' Nevertheless, a more fundamentalist group of individuals answered Shearer's call to arms.

Andrew Kerr and those at the Bell & Scott office were bombarded with death threats, curses and apocalyptic omens. Every day for months the post would arrive with a new wave

---

1 Rutland Court, Edinburgh (Anderson Strathern)

Following the merger of Strathern & Blair and J&F Anderson it became increasingly impractical to remain based in the premises at Castle Street and Charlotte Street. In 2004 Anderson Strathern relocated to 1 Rutland Court in the heart of the city's financial district. Over 200 people work over its several floors, with the top-floor conference and meeting space commanding impressive views of the city and castle. During modernisation of the office space in 2017 a number of documents were unearthed among a staggering 15.3 tonnes of paper, 9.36 tonnes of metal and 3.2 tonnes of wood that were cleared and recycled.

The office reception, accessible from a walkway which features a statue of a bucking horse by Eoghan Bridge, houses three recently unlocked iron chests and several other artefacts from the firm's history.

of unabridged hatred, each with a damning indictment on the souls of all involved. Years later, Kerr recalled the perseverance of one group of Welsh Baptists in particular, who had managed to track down detailed information about the law firm and its employees. Luckily for all involved, in the face of overwhelming support from both Christians and the public at large, the call for censorship soon fell apart, and the Bible Board was vindicated in their action. Eventually, the Pocket Canons were translated into twelve different languages, leading to a global distribution of millions.

As the merged firm entered its fourth century, a break from the past was finally confronted. After around 200 years of occupation of Charlotte Street and Castle Street, the premises were deemed impractical and constrictive. Plans were put in place for a move out of the historical offices into a new building in Edinburgh's financial district at Rutland Court. From the top floor, the New Town offices of John Gibson, Alexander Duncan and John Inglis are visible, as is the western prospect

---

George House, Glasgow (Anderson Strathern)

The firm's Glasgow operations moved to this location on Glasgow's George Square in one of several quick expansions as Anderson Strathern sought to provide a Scotland-wide service covering the entirety of Scotland. Following an initial move in 2005, the 2008 acquisition of Kerr & Co. necessitated a move to larger premises, this time in the centre of the city at George Square. The modern office has excellent views of the neoclassical City Chambers and is just a stone's throw from the main buildings of the University of Strathclyde and City of Glasgow College. The centrepiece of the square is a statue of Sir Walter Scott, a former client, who gazes back down at the law firm from his 80-foot-high pedestal.

of Edinburgh Castle, the site of John Davidson's Old Town practice. Into this modern glass building were heaved three locked iron chests, the sole survivors of a lineage stretching back to a distant past.

Afterword

From monk to notary to writer to solicitor. From Adomnán mac Rónán to John Skene to Alexander Duncan to Rosemary Mackenzie. Throughout history, many have seen their own times as an improvement upon the past, with society and the law in a constant state of progress. The worlds and works of the individuals uncovered in this book suggest the law is rarely linear.

Hundreds of years after the creation of the Law of the Innocents, John Skene was ordering the execution of innocent women on grounds of witchcraft. Opportunities of advancement fostered by the Scottish Enlightenment were succeeded by stagnant social stratification. When that system finally fell it was not by means of peaceful progress but by the collective trauma brought on by the advent of total warfare. Today, recently won rights require a constant defence.

Not only have the buildings, faces, clients and laws changed, but the ideas and practices through which they have operated have too. While technological innovation, public service and an active role in shaping Scots law have generally persisted, they alone do not constitute the real essence of the legal community. A historical partnership is a sum of its people: a random assortment of names, strangers in their lifetimes, separated by time and traditions, joined by a thin thread of association only tied together in the present. Each generation enriches the story of the present, contributes a material legacy of buildings, letters and clients, and reaffirms the reputation hard won by those who went before.

In some ways living up to this ideal is easier today; in other ways it is more difficult. With the penetration of technology into every aspect of life, the primacy of the office is on the decline, making possible a return to the style of the largely itinerant practices of John Davidson and Alexander Duncan. As is evident throughout this history, failing to adapt to such changes often leads to a failure to survive, and flexibility is vital.

We have journeyed through three very different eras in the evolution of a Scottish law firm. The first was the business of the lone practitioner, perhaps with an apprentice or junior partner, depending upon private clients and the Crown. The second witnessed management of historical practices by legal dynasties, passing the business through sons, fathers, nephews and cousins and generally expanding in line with the increasing complexity of everyday life. The third saw a move away from familial networks towards a more meritocratic structure of management, increasing the trajectory of growth and decreasing the reliance on tradition. The human condition, epitomised in those emotionally charged moments of seduction, sedition and subterfuge, unites them.

In each era, huge changes in Scottish society meant law firms had to change and adapt. In the time of Davidson, a Calvinist, feudal Scotland confronted the enlightened ideas of a society built on tolerance, reason and a separation of Church and State. In the time of Gibson, the application of many Enlightenment ideas concerning commerce and capital demanded a reimagining of Scotland's place in the Union. The last great shudder came with the collapse of the Victorian edifice of imperial self-confidence, with a traditionalist society giving way to one that not only embraced diversity, but defined itself by it. Although this is a simplification of the trends witnessed in these eras, it gives a sense of a nation in a constant state of flux, ever redefining itself.

We can wonder if the world might have been slightly different had John Davidson not provided Adam Smith, James Hutton and others with the research necessary to construct their revolutionary theories, or John Gibson had not defended, for the first time, the intellectual property of his client, or Arthur Russell had not secured so many of Scotland's natural treasures. Without people like John Inglis and Rosemary Mackenzie, the practical operation of the law at times of unparalleled crisis and growth would have been impossible. The spirit of the law can change, but its past remains fixed in the letters of the law.

PART 2

LETTERS OF THE LAW

Edward, Earl of Conway: Letter from the Court of Charles II to Ireland (1681)

This brief letter sent from an Anglo-Irish noble to his brother gives a short but interesting insight into the machinations of the Court of Charles II before the controversial ascension to the throne of his Catholic brother James VII and II. Here, in very concise terms, we see Conway describing his position at Court, including his wife's elevation to the Queen's Bedchamber, as well as explanations of military manoeuvres in Luxembourg. As noted elsewhere, Edward, Earl of Conway, was the Secretary of State for the Northern Department at this time, having responsibility for foreign relations with northern Protestant Europe. We might also speculate that the 'Mr Farewell' whom the letter mentions could be James Farewell, an English poet and writer of the time, albeit only 16 years of age at the time of writing. The text below has been transcribed with the now archaic spelling and grammar intact.

Whitehall, 6th December 1681

Deare Brother,

I am very glad to heare you are so well able to undertake a Journey to Drogheda, and to Dublin. If your sonne Arthur likes Sr James Grahams Daughter, I think they have noreason to make difficultys, or exceptions to what you propose.

The Draft which Mr Farewell hath sent me shall be dispatcht to morrow, the King went yesterday to Windsor and doth not returne till to morrow night.

I have acquainted my Cousin Gavin with your Project about concealed Lands, and your intention to divide with him, upon which account he will be ready to solicit that affaire when it shall properly come heere, But it must take its course, and have its first Reference to my Lord Lieutenent of Ireland, which I have transmitted to you by this Post that you may loose no time, when it returnes it must be referd to the Lords of the Treasury, before it comes to the King.

This afternoone my Wife was sworne one of the Ladys of the Bed Chamber to the Queen.

Our great affaires heere depend upon removing the forse which the French use about Luxembourg, and if it be not removed, it will certainly necessitate his Majesty to call a Parliament.

I doe not mention the Proceedings upon Farming the Revenue of Ireland, because that is not concluded, and I think the King is very indifferent in the matter, but there are those that lay great weight upon it how they come to be so engaged I know not.

The King hath declared the Duke of Richmond Master of the Horse to the great mortification of the Duke of Monmouth.

There hath been great discourse in this Towne of the Duke of Yorkes returne to Court, but there is nothing of it.

If this meets you at Dublin, I desire you to reminde my Lord Lieut: of his promise to gratifie me in the choise of my Lieutenant at Charlemount, without which I can have no satisfaction in doing what I ought to doe for the good of that place. My Lord of Arran lately assured me he would write to my Lord Lieutenant about it. Pray present my humble service to my Lord Granard, and assure him that I am not in the least afraid in my respect and friendship to his Lordship and that I long extremely both to heare from him and see him. So I rest.

Your entirely affectionate brother,

Conway

2.2

Reverend Dan McAuley: Letter on Requirement to Reform the Highlands (1725)

This emotive letter captures the dire conditions, and hostile reception, which Presbyterian ministers met in the Scottish Highlands between the two Jacobite rebellions. The vast jurisdiction covered in this letter, the Synod of Glenelg, covered the Isles of Skye, Lewis and Harris as well as swathes of the Western Highlands. Synods, or Provincial Synods, were courts of the Church of Scotland that came between presbyteries and the General Assembly; this letter is a report from the Synod of Glenelg to the General Assembly in Edinburgh. Having been written before the full onset of General Wade's construction of an extensive network of roads and forts, we find in this letter valuable and rare detail of life in the Highlands before extensive external involvement. We are also afforded some very frank descriptions of the attitudes of Highlanders to the Kirk, though the extremity of the treatment of the ministry may have been exaggerated in an attempt to secure funds for improving their condition.

Very Reverend Dear Brethren,

We have met Synodically in this place according to the appointment of the General Assembly in a peaceable manner in the name of the Lord Jesus Christ the allowed King and Head of his Church, under the protection of our gracious Sovereign King George, and we desire to acknowledge the good providence of God therein, and we bless His Name for the hopes we have of being enabled through his grace, under the kind influence of our only rightful and lawful kings auspicious reign, to carry on a reformation in the vast bounds committed to our charge. We received the Assembly's letter with the Act for Reformation of the Highlands and Islands and cannot but with thankful hearts acknowledge His Majesty's royal bounty for maintaining itinerant preachers and catechists in these parts, where popery and ignorance abound; we have also received an extract of the Committee's Act about the Distribution of His Majesty's foresaid Bounty, and when we consider the same we judge that the state of our bounds hath not been fully under the consideration of the honourable and reverend members of that Committee, and this we think may be occasioned by the absence of our members from it, and by the activity and forwardness of others present.

We therefore now beg leave to inform you that our bounds are of vast extent, being no less than 400 miles in circumference, having only 20 ministerial charges: some of our parishes are 40, some 30 and some 10 miles in length and near as many in breadth; few of our people know letters; popery abounds, yea and flourishes in several parishes among us, and there are some places where the Reformation never to this day had any footing; our work is great, difficult and dangerous, and the labourers are few, our worldly encouragement very small, few friends and many enemies; we want the assistance of judges and magistrates as others have, very few of us have glebes or manses and many of us want roofed churches and are obliged to wander from corner to corner to preach in the open air to the great detriment of our health, the marks of which are visible in our extenuated bodies. Some of us have no Decrees for our stipend but are at the mercy of those liable for the payment thereof and generally have it to take up in smalls from the people, the generality of which are miserably poor, who if they had been in other places, would appear to be, as they are really, objects of charity, which brings them to look upon our ministry as a burden. But if ministers were in case to use hospitality, without ruining their families, they would be more culpable, nay it is found by experience that without keeping open families our presence and ministry would be despised.

There are no schools in our bounds except such as The Honourable Society for Propagating Christian Knowledge maintains.

From this short account of the state of our bounds His Majesty's royal grant seems to point directly only, and to be chiefly designed for us if the clamor causa have a better hearing than clamor personarum, which we cannot question in your management, and therefore we can without the imputation of selfishness expect that those places and parishes which are but 2, 3, 3 or 5 miles long and fully planted and where they have or might have schools and where ministers have large stipends, glebes, manses and churches, and civil magistrates at hand to protect them and strengthen their lands, should not put on a level with us in the rank of objects of help and commiseration. Some of us have borne under such discouragements that we are now like to faint, and had struggled within ourselves what to do, but our Gracious Sovereign showing such a remarkable concern for promoting the interest of religion in his gracious letter to the General Assembly, did revive our spirits and add more vigour to our endeavours, so that we resolved on a new essay, and notwithstanding that some of us, more through fatigue and constant toil than age, are tender, yet all of our number came to the Synod except two, and when we came to the place of meeting we were long kindly entertained by that worthy gentleman who commanded the Garrison of the place, Captain Johnston; the last beam of the influence of His Majesty's Government is sweet unto us; our meeting at this Synod though troublesome and expensive we hope may be found to God's glory: for we have resolved that our work be great and difficulties many, yet the cause being good and our gracious God faithful in his promises, and our earthly Sovereign as almost a nursing father to his church having concerned himself therein, which is our greatest encouragement under God, to go on in the work in the strength of Christ the Lord and Master of the harvest.

We lay our account with opposition but from none except such as are enemies to our gracious Sovereigns person and government. We think that we cannot in faithfulness to our God and King but show that the want of civil magistrates in our bounds does very great prejudice to the interest of religion as well as to His Majesty's service. We in the isles have no sheriffs nearer than Inverness or Ross which be at a great distance from us, nor any Justice of the Peace except one in the whole Isle of Skye which is no less than 40 miles in length, nor any in the Long Island which is 72 miles long, no Judge or Parish Ballie in the Lews or the west of the Long Island excepting very few. We therefore intreat that the Reverend and Honourable Commission of the General Assembly or the Committee for Managing His Majesty's Bounty, may apply to His Majesty or other proper persons under the King to nominate Justices of the Peace in the isles of Skye, Lews and the west of the Long Island and in the countries which formerly belonged to the late Earl of Seaforth, and commission parochial Ballies in the Lews and other places above mentioned and apply to the Lords Commissioners of the Treasury and Barons of Exchequer to ordain payment of ministers stipends, and that they be provided with roofed churches, manses, glebes and grain according to law, and that a school be settled in each parish of the Lews.

We do complain that none of the correspondence from the Reverend Synods of Argyll and Ross came to our recent Synod which was very discouraging to us, and we hope the Commissioners will take notice thereof.

We humbly propose that more itinerant preachers and catechists may be ordered for us in the time to come, and that Mr John McLeod, now on trials, when he is licensed to preach may be one of them. As to what you wrote concerning the [illegible] it lies at a great distance from us and we agree that there be a new Presbytery erected in Strathnaver and that the Presbyteries of Strathnaver, Dornoch and Caithness be erected into a Synod by themselves.

This in name and by appointment of the Synod of Glenelg is subscribed by Very R. D. B. your affectionate brother and servant in the Lord

Glenelg

July 12th

1725   Dan McAulay – Moderator

2.3

Adam Smith: Dispensation and Assignation
to Robert Balfour Ramsay (1754)

Possibly the most significant item discovered in connection with this history was a 1754 dispensation and assignation detailing a previously unknown court battle which took place in the early life of the economist and philosopher Adam Smith. Overall, the document settles a conflict between Smith and Margaret Balfour over heritable bonds and rents in Fife which Smith had inherited from his late father, with Balfour's relative Robert Balfour Ramsay effectively taking on the debt and purchasing Smith's share of lands and rents. Running to 15 pages, it details events spanning 1733 through to 1754, including a case at the Court of Session in 1748, and includes annotations by Smith himself on some pages. With a great deal of Smith's correspondence and documentation destroyed at his request following his death, this is a valuable insight into a potentially important and formative process in his very early life. To give a taste of the legalese of the mid eighteenth century, the first and final pages of the document are transcribed below. The text below has been transcribed with the now archaic spelling and grammar intact.

Page 1: Be it Known to all men by these presents, me Adam Smith lawful son of the deceased Adam Smith late Comptroller of the Customs at Kirkcaldy, now one of the Professor of Philosophy in the University of Glasgow; Forasmuch as Mrs Margaret Balfour Eldest Daughter of the deceased Robert Lord Burleigh by her bond dated the seventh day of February One Thousand Seven Hundred and Thirty Three years granted her to have borrowed and received at the term of Candlemas then last notwithstanding the date of the said bond from the persons therein named my Tutor upon account of me their pupil, all and whole the sum of Four thousand merks scots money, which sum the said Mrs Margaret Balfour bound and obliged her, her heir extow and successor to content and repay to me and my said Tutor on my account and my heirs or assignor at and against the term of Lambas then next, with the sum of Eight hundred merks money foresaid of liquidate penalty in case of fatality, Together with the due and ordinary sent of the said principal sum yearly termly and proportionally so long as the same should remain unpaid, and for further security to me and my foresaids and my said Tutor around the premassex and by hurt or prejudice to the foresaid personal obligement. The said Mrs Margaret Balfour, bound and obliged her and her foresaids to infess and leave me and my foresaids upon her own proper charges and expenses in an eent of Two hundred merks or such eents as shall correspond by the Laws of Scotland for the time to the foresaid principal sum of Four Thousand Merks yearly to be uplifted and taken at two terms in the year, Lambas and Candlemass by equal portions forth of all and haill the town and lands of Demperstoun Easter and towards Shilboland and Shiboland and that part called Walkerland with parts pendidex annexes coonnexex Dependencies Outside such tenants tenantries and services of free tenants of the same with all their testaments, all lying within the parish of Auchtermuchty and Sheriffdom of Fife and which are parts and pertinents of the Barony of Strathmiglo, or forth of any part of the portion of the said lands readiesh malls

Page 15: My Piors and Attour I hereby devise and require and each of you constitute and seally my bailies in that part hereby specially constitute that on sight hereof ye pass to the ground of the said lands of demperstoun, Shilboland, Shiboland and walkerland and there give heritable state and sasine real actual and corporal possession of all and whole the foresaid amount of two hundred merks or such amount less or more as shall by law correspond for the time to the foresaid principal sum of four thousand merks scots money yearly to be uplifted and taken at the said two terms of Lambass and Candlemass by equal portions worth of all and whole the said toun and lands of Demperstoun Easter and Wester, Shilboland and Shiboland, and that part called Walkerland, with the pertinents lying aforesaid and which and parts and pertinents of the said lands and Barony of Strathmiglo or forth of any part or portion of the said lands readiest Maills farms profits and duties of the same to be holder and under revision in [document damaged] mention in the said heritable bond to the said Robert Balfour Ramsay and his foresaids by the delivery to him or them or their certain attorney in their name bearer hereof Earth and Stone of the grounds of the said lands a penny money and other usual symbols and this in no ways ye have undone. The which to do I commend to you to continue and seally as said in my full power by this my precept of sasine directed to you for that affect. In witness whereof I have subserved there presents consenting of this and the fourteen preceding pages wrote upon stamped paper by William Robertson clerk to James Graham Writer to the Signet for all Glasgow the Fourth day of January one Thousand seven hundred and fifty four years before these witnesses the honourable Alexander Gordon son to the deceased William Earl of Aberdeen and James Sloan my Servant Witness also to my subscribing the marginal note on the twelfth page wrote by the said William Robertson

Signed Alex Gordon, James Sloan, Adam Smith

James Beck: 'The Garden of Dorantes' (1770)

Among the most bizarre documents found in the course of this investigation are the short stories of James Beck, an apprentice and later client of one of Anderson Strathern's historical practices. While we have already made mention of these stories more broadly, it was this one, 'The Garden of Dorantes', that Beck appears to have been most proud of and is therefore presented here in full. Unlike the other stories, the sex and scandal of the upper middle class is dropped in favour of a more philosophical investigation of the stadial progress of human nature; while less revealing of the domestic thoughts and whims of his class, it is enlightening as regards contemporary attitudes towards the natural world, religion, gender roles and death. The paper on which these stories were written shows almost no sign of age, appearing to all intents and purposes as though it was written upon yesterday. This makes these pages remarkable to observe and handle, but it also suggests that centuries may have passed without a single person reading the stories they contained. The text below has been transcribed with the archaic spelling and grammar intact.

Alexis to Propertius

Dear Friend,

I am now on a visit to the sensible and benevolent Dorantes. You are no stranger to the history of my Friend. He now enjoys all the philosophic ease and grateful tranquility a good conscience, an extensive experience, numerous friends and plentiful fortune can yield to a cultivated mind. He was long tossed in the tumultuous and troublesome scenes of life, these storms are now over, and he waits with true christian hope in the recesses of the most beautiful retirement imaginable for that hour which is to set him free from mortality. It was in consequence of repeated invitations I made this little jaunt, prevented by unavoidable business I could not accept them before this time. When I arrived at the Seat of Dorantes I found what I was sure of receiving, an hearty welcome, the most friendly treatment imaginable, attended with unaffected freedom and ease, and every agreeable rule of real and true hospitality.

The House is antique, commodious and large; commanding a noble and unequaled prospect over a great extent of the adjoining County, and the meandering neighbouring River. The whole is remarkably fine particularly the situation, and the air there abouts is healthy and pure. Near to the old mansion are Gardens of considerable extent, well laid out, and in a taste peculiarly expressive of the good understanding of the owner of them, they are furnished with every thing necessary for either pleasure, ornament, or use. A Park well stocked with Deer circumscribed the Gardens, while they again were surrounded with an hunting Forest, which reached to the bottom of a ridge of very high hills bounding the view towards the north.

Within this forest was an immense inclosure, surrounded with an exceedingly high wall comprehending many acres of ground, and seemed to be intended for some very particular purpose which at first I could not discover. The unthinking part of mankind have long reckoned our Friend Dorantes a humourist, while but a few know him to be a man of the most finished taste, and cultivated an understanding as any in Europe; the sequel of this letter will corroborate the truth of this assertion. I well know that for many years he had been a great lover of what is called Virtue, and had improved his knowledge of the fine arts at a prodigious expense, but not before this visit to him in the Country was I acquainted with the particular use he intended all the Paintings and Statues for he had been collecting with the utmost care.

On the forenoon of the second day after my arrival I was rambling in the Forest with Dorantes, and could not help asking him what that large Inclosure incased. He answered with a smile that there was inclosed with the wall then before us a scene which many would esteem to be the effect of a distempered imagination, but in fact, it was solely the work of fancy to improve reflection and promote rational amusement. You will easily imagine my curiosity was sufficiently raised to beg my kind Host would immediately satisfy it; this, I no sooner mentioned as my wish than in the most obliging manner he complied.

Putting out a key from his pocket he begged me to follow him, I did so with the most anxious expectation, and in a few minutes led me into a place wonderful and surprising indeed. Dorantes locked the door after we were entered; observing my astonishment he took me by the hand and said what think you of this my young Friend? You see before you the work of twenty years labour and at the expense of a sixth part of the large Fortune I possess. Do not the whole seem to be the offspring of folly? You're emotion marks your opinion. I replied hastily my countenance belies my sentiments if it gives you reason to judge as you speak; my heart is filled with wonder, but it is the wonder of admiration and involuntary applause seeing I am neither acquainted with what is now before me, or in the cause in you which gave rise to the object of my amazement. What means what I see? These four grand divisions! These winding and variegated walks, these Pictures, these Statues, and that Temple at the farthest end of the whole? Have patience a little my youthful Sir, not so fast Alexis, replied Dorantes, let us move slowly on at this time, and before you leave the country, I shall have opportunities sufficient to explain to you the design and meaning of what now creates in you so much surprise. I have of late more complied with my fancy than my judgement in the disposal of a large part of my fortune, which you well know is very considerable; the scene now before you is a glaring proof of how much my imagination takes the lead at least in this instance.

Soon after I had quitted all my Employments under the State, with a determined resolution never more to engage in busy scenes, I divided this spot from the remainder of the Forest, and formed it into the shape and fashion you now see, merely in compliance with a whimsical inclination I had formed for some time before, of realising a train of reflections on the beginning and ending of mortal existence.

I call the long walk before you the walk through life. You may observe I have portioned it out into four spaces, each of them is assigned to a grand division of the life of Man as successively distinguished by Childhood, Youth, Manhood, and old Age. The windings and turnings I made should represent the pursuits, errors, and different ways of Mankind; yonder Temple finishes the scene, and winds up the role of misery and human life. Knowledge but encreased my surprise and admiration: I wondered at the grandeur, the goodness of the genius of my Friend. I expressed in the warmest terms the pleasure I at that moment felt, gave the palm to Judgement, and observed that the height of this principle could only produce the original Ideas of such noble Images as were then in view, and allowed the utmost heat of fancy and warmth of imagination but as secondary causes in the formation of so delightful a place. Dorantes thanked me for the flattering preference I gave to judgement at the same time mentioned his fears that a nearer inspection into the execution of his design would prove this preference but a mere compliment. I frankly staked my opinion against his fears, and we proceeded to the tryal.

Immediately within the wall everything bore an exact resemblance to the primitive ages of the world. Here, wild and uncultivated nature reigned triumphant, neither art nor science had yet dared to rein in her extravagance, nor the vanity of Man appeared under the figure of improvement. In this part Large Trees were placed without any apparent order or design, and were indiscriminately mixed with Bushes and Briars, which owed nothing to the hand of culture. A few troubled Streams were visible among their roots, changing along their unwilling waters, the prey of stagnation and the primitive inertia of matter. Here and there could be seen the appearance of savage Beasts either watching their prey, or couching in their dens; no paths were visible in this wilderness but were supposed to have been made by them. This was the world said my Conductor before Man was created! Before Heaven had finished it's handywork in the perfection of the whole, Earth was adorned as you see by confusion and inequality, savage fierceness and appetite were unable to produce order; the souls of Man must be first produced alone capable of restraining the wild sallies of nature.

As Dorantes spoke we advanced, almost imperceptible losing the rudness of the earliest times, in the approaching view we began to discover a more cultivated spot descriptive as well of the childhood of man, as the infancy of Science. Here, nature began to form a more pleasing appearance and cultivated form as the arts (tho' yet in their infancy), were seen employed pruning here luxuriances and prescribing bounds to her before unlimited powers. An image of the Spring of exquisite workmanship stood at the entrance of this division smiling at Childhood and Innocence playing at her feet, while she directed Generation who, under the figure of a Sower was busy but at a little distance from her. Spring bore the exact image of the beautiful Emilliana, all the living charms of the little divinity were displayed. I was just about to seize her in my arms when the coldness of the Marble convinced me that the enchanting fire and vivacity of the fair original were wanting to animate the stone and warm it into life. Dorantes smiled at my emotion and beckoned me away. I followed slowly, absorbed in contemplation, viewing with eager eyes all the objects that surrounded me on every side. I could perceive the most beautiful and variegated Flowers and Shrubs covered the Plains and little Meadows which this portion was divided with great natural simplicity, interspersed with glowing Insects and gaudy colloured Butterflies, which seems to fly from as pursued by numbers of little Children scattered everywhere about employed in such pursuits, while others were playing with the Lamb or Kid sporting about the banks of the clear transparent Riverlets watering this delicious spot, filled with innumerable small, but fishes of the most beautiful tints and what alone had real life, although every Figure in the place imposed upon the sight as appearing to be actually alive so highly finished were they all by the Statuary. The whole scene breathed nothing but infant nature, the Birds were just hatching their young, the Flowers buding, the Plants blossoming, the fruit on the Trees were just set, and the Trees themselves of but a few years growth.

There was a Figure for almost every childish amusement executed with great judgement and taste, so naturally placed, and in such easy attitudes, that you could perceive the apparent difference of dispositions in even the infantile state; and the unequal approaches from childhood to Youth were visible as we walked along, and more strongly marked every step we went. Around these puerile scenes were several Groves and Dens of various dimensions, and adorned with Pictures by the very best hands. I entered into one of them and found it dedicated to Hymen, who was lighting up his torch to give happiness complete to a new married couple, while the generating Power was about to diffuse his genial influence over the connubial bed. This was supported by two pieces in smaller frames, the one representing a fond Husband allowed to thank his Spouse for the present of a fine Boy; the other, a Mother suckling her child. The manly gratitude in the Husband mingled with emotions of the most ardent affection were peculiarly striking; and only to be equaled by the strongest expression of maternal fondness in the delighted Mother with the lovely Babe at her breast. Here, weded love had both its birth and reward.

The near resemblance of the Figures then before me to certain persons whom we both know, made me imagine they were all drawn from the life, in this conjecture I was afterwards confirmed. Dorantes in these Gardens gave the virtues of his Friends a a noble monument of his esteem. Cleomedon was not less tenderly affectionate in this little Temple dedicated to that God who had completely blessed him by joining him forever to his beloved and charming Melliora, than in his own house. She adored her kneeling Husband, yet could only steal a look now and then from the sweet Babe, who seemed to smile at the perfect happiness of its parents. You are no stranger to the vast fondness of Melliora for her Children, I even thought it inexpressible till now. The Painter did it justice, and marked her one of the most amiable of women.

A little way beyond this on the other side was a Grot sacred to what is called natural-affection. She is represented as if assisting at the work of creation bestowing certain fixed and inalterable principles upon the Brutes, which is called instinct, but mixing with the mortal mould an affection variable and inconstant yet far superior in essence and beauty to what she gave the beasts. This Grot was adorned with two large pieces of painting, one on each side of it. That on the right was an enraged Lioness defending her cubs from the attack of a multitude of Hunters with incredible fury, and apparent success. She had already brought several of them to the ground mangled in a terrible manner, the rest were just about to fly. The savage Heroine had one eye fixed on her enemies, the other looked askance towards her den; to this and her Cubs the genius of Instinct pointed with her finger animating the furious Dam with new vigour and strength. In this picture Dorantes gave the praise due to that instinctive principle every Beast invariably obeys nor is it ever fickle or inconsistent; in the other (on the left hand) was a severe but too just reproach on human kind.

Here, natural-affection was fled, for a woman was seen just returned from the inhuman act of exposing her new born Babe, which lay in a thicket just a little distance from her. False-shame under the figure of a Fury had first tempted the unhappy Creature to the perpetration of this diabolical deed, and like a true devil was now punishing her for it, by holding up before her a reflective glass in which was seen Guilt produced in the most hideous colours horror could invent, and far beyond what imagination can conceive. The wretched fugitive wished now to fly from herself, but Reflection assisted the Fury in ever presenting before her eyes the guilty sight, at the same time they were ever pushing her towards the gulf of Misery, where, Dispair, brandishing a dreadful scourge was ready to receive her. I quickly turned my eyes from this shocking scene of human wretchedness; they were instantly filled with tears on sight of so just and affecting representation of the beautiful yet guilty Messalina. Dorantes had done everything in his power to save her from perdition, but we all fear from her own horrid exit, his charitable pains were without effect.

Observing my too visible emotion he hurried me from hence; the open walk of Life helped to dissipate the disagreeable impression guilt had occasioned, and I soon after recovered my wonted tranquility. After this we went through several walks full of the finest reflections on the infancy of Man, each Figure conveyed a moral lesson told in such a manner as lessons were never told before. We had not gone a great way however before I stopped short at the entrance of a Grove of Cypess and of Yill. My Conductor immediately read in my eyes my desire of exploring this winding retreat, he entered, and I followed.

The turnings of this Grove were so peculiarly laid out as by insensible degrees to impress upon the mind a melancholy, gentle and sad, judiciously intended as a proper introduction to what was to follow. As Dorantes walked along without my perceiving it, he touched a string. Imagine my surprise when on a sudden I heard musick begin of the softest and most soothing strains, I continued in some time in silent rapture, nor had power to move until the musick ceased. When advancing a few steps farther in too the middle of the Grove, my soft surprise was transformed into an awful admiration, accompanied by the strongest sense of pity and grief – This was the House of Sorrow – a female Figure of black marble noble and majestic filled the farther end; seated on a throne in the shape of a human heart. From her my eyes were soon imperceptibly drawn to a Figure then paying adorations to the Alter, who struck me in the most interesting manner. This was a Mother lamenting the premature death of her first born

Child. The Mother was the incomparable Mira herself. The utmost dignity of grief was here displayed, in the most masterly manner I ever yet beheld; all the luxury of inconceivable distress was present. The silent inexpressible anguish of the fair Mourner was finely imitated. Ah Propertius had you been with me you had died, your soul must have fled into the figure of your favourite and once much loved Mistress. With the last heart rending kiss she imprints upon the clay cold lips of the little Leonline her whole soul struggles for freedom that it might follow her lost and much loved Infant. The Spirit now freed from life, conducted by Innocence, is seen in its flight towards the mansions of the blessed, Heaven opens its wide extended gates, and the Angels with joyful songs seem to welcome the happy guest. Here, I could have looked whole hours away; the unavoidable distress mitigated the pain; the well known form of the charming Mira, which shone brightest in the deepest shades, recalled a pleasing altho' melancholy recollection, and in this, Propertius, you was joined. The prospect of Immortal felicity admirably thrown in by the Artist, in some little measure alleviated the sting of the deep misfortune of the short life of the infant Leonline, it seemed to diffuse a faint gleam of satisfaction oer the countenance of the longing Mother, otherwise covered with unutterable woe.

Dorantes interrupted my reverie, and leading me away from this moving scene, was advancing fast from the last stages of Childhood towards the precinct of Youth, when observing the morning was far advanced, he mentioned breakfast would be upon the table and proposed returning immediately for fear that Amelia should be alarmed at our late stay abroad. I complied, on his promise to embrace the earliest opportunity of attending me through the remainder of this wonderful place.

Was I only to mention every beauty this puerile but delightful scene offered to the most transient view, I must send you my friend a volume and not a letter. The exquisite judgement of the whole design was beyond description; the execution was not less praise worthy; and the effect strong and visible upon every beholder. The Statues, the walks, the Hedges, the very bushes filled with the nests of a variety of singing Birds were all analogous to, and highly expressive of the infancy of Man, of his Childhood, and of his earliest State. The whole displayed such a true picture of childish simplicity and native innocence as the whole warmth of the most refined fancy could not improve.

Absorbed in such pleasing reflections we reached the House, where you'll suppose me seated at breakfast with one of the most amiable Women, and sensible Men in all England, a feast that can be but in very few places equalled, and no where excelled. With them you must leave me until I have an opportunity of writing to you again, which shall be soon I promise you, seeing nothing gives me so much pleasure as assuring you I certainly am with the utmost Gleem,

Dear Sir;

Your humble Servant and most faithful Friend,

Bucks, 1770

Alexis

Alexander MacKrabie: The Journal of Messrs Francis and MacKrabie (1774)

This short diary, found amidst the papers of Alexander Duncan, details the voyage of Phillip Francis, a member of the Supreme Council of Bengal, and his brother-in-law Alexander MacKrabie as they travel to India for the first time. En route to Calcutta, they encounter customs and traditions among Dutch settlers in Cape Town, Islamic islanders in the Indian Ocean and wealthy Nawabs along the eastern coast of India. The existence of the diary is itself a conundrum – a slightly different version appears in printed form in 'The Francis Letters' – meaning that this version is either the original made during the voyage or a copy made retrospectively by MacKrabie. With its inconsistent flow, matter-of-factness and rushed ending it may be the former. The diary also seems to have made its way into Duncan's possession directly from MacKrabie, as the two were in correspondence at the time of the voyage. As was the case with the passage of James Beck's personal documents to Duncan in 1788, the diary may have passed to Duncan upon MacKrabie's premature death in 1778. The text below has been transcribed with the now archaic spelling and grammar intact.

March 30th 1774: At 9 in the evening, set off from Duke Street Westminster and at 11 arrived at Epsom worn out with every possible fatigue of body and mind. Sleep is a sovereign cordial in these cases and we took a large dose of it. After breakfast next morning proceed by way of Guildford, Liphook and Petersfield. We had little to boast of in the course of this day's journey except good weather and better spirits – neither food near horses were to be got but at the expense 2 hours delay at each stage. At 9 our Chaise set us down at the Kings Arms in Portsmouth where we bid adieu to that mode of travelling for some years. The innkeeper and his household seemed no way insensible of the honours due to an East India counsellor and we foresaw his bill would be of the very first rank.

April 1st 1774: Colonel Monson paid Mr Francis a visit in order to settle the plan of embarkation – we were all invited to dine on board a 64 gunship the Worcester. At 5 in the afternoon the commissioners yacht conveyed us through a storm of wind and rain and after half an hour's sailing we found ourselves in safely on board the Ashburnham at Spithead where we met general Clavering and his family – all sick. We had ample room for meditation and little enough for exercise. Nothing could exceed either the crowd or the noise of this cursed ship. When the first confusion had a little subsided and we had turned every square inch of space of our cabins to some purpose of convenience it was judged incumbent on us to form rules for maintaining a proper decorum in the course of the little trip we looked forward to. Every article relative to our meals, the hours at which we should take them, and the ceremonies, necessary to be observed on all occasions, being thoroughly, we began to think it high time to take our departure, but the god of winds was no less inclined to delay our voyage, after we left London, than the worthy proprietors of India stock shewed themselves before it. After 10 days he relented and on the 12th of April vouchsafed us an Easterly breeze under the influence of which we set sail and in a few hours lost sight of England. To make a voyage thoroughly interesting it is supposed necessary that the Passengers should quarrel everyday, this however, forming no part of our system, the run to Madeira had nothing extraordinary in it except it's being performed in 9 days.

21st April 1774: On the 21st of April, we came to an anchor in Fonchall Bay and landed the next morning. Our friends on board the Anson had the start of us by a few hours. Madiera, Proto, Santo, and some other rocks in the Neighbourhood, although they were at the Hesperides, the insule Atlantis, and the Seat of the Elysium of the ancients; and even though the good folks of these degenerate days, find in them a comfortable place of refreshment after the fatigues of a voyage; yet we hope it will by no means be understood, that a man may pass his time pleasantly there for a fortnight. We were overcome with civilities and embarked again with a degree of rapture – upon the 1st of May – having contributed to the Honour of Happiness of the British Factory by a display of more beauty than ever landed among them, and to their profit by an immense export of wine for the use of our families in India. I make them no allowance upon the score of our eating, as the fleas and mosquitos took care to make ample reprisals.

3rd May 1774: On the 3rd of May at noon we discovered the snowy summit of Teneriffe. It continued a very visible object during the course of above a hundred and fifty miles sailing. After keeping company with the Anson till the 27th of May, we lost sight of her unaccountably.

29th May 1774: On the 29th we crossed the line, but were not sensible of any extraordinary effect it had either upon our persons or principles. June 4th being the King's birthday was observed with a proper degree of solemnity – his good subjects in the cabin drank his health in full bribers – those in the steerage followed our example with great zeal; but their loyalty getting the better of their discretion, some of the sailors passed the night in irons. The occupations or reflections of a man who lives six months upon the ocean afford little entertainment either to himself or his friends when he gets on shore. We catch sharks and lose patience – compose verses and knit garters – but in spite of vexation, continued in perfect health all the time, though neither that nor fair weather can make such a voyage comfortable. People who pray for long life, have it in their power to live as long as they think proper. They need only go to sea to turn seconds into centuries.

3rd July 1774: On the 3rd of July we arrived at the Cape of Good Hope – and at midnight came to anchor at False

Bay – though it was the depth of winter in the southern hemisphere – though the dutch settlement at the cape is but a barren region at best – and False Bay the very worst part of it – our impatience carried us on shore by day break the next morning. After suffering endless extortion in the article of wagons and horses and enduring hunger and cold and weariness, during a journey of twenty five miles, we reached Cape Town, the capital. The Governor and other principal inhabitants treated us with the marks of the greatest politeness and respect. They made balls, concerts and splendid suppers for our entertainment, but conversation is impractical in a dutch settlement. The people are so silent and uniform in themselves, and so perfectly indifferent about what happens out of themselves, that we found the difference of language of very little consequence to us. It was not quite so easy to reconcile ourselves to their climate and customs – a damp, cold air, and no warmth except that of a charcoal stove – large houses with bare walls and brick floors – we absolutely went to bed in the middle of the day to avoid perishing! Of the natural history of the country, I have only to observe that there certainly are such animals as ostriches, zebras, hottentots and sea lions, and with respect to dutch police, I can assure you that a man may be as effectively impaled at the cape of good hope, as in Constantinople.

18th July 1774: We left the Cape of Good Hope in the 18th of July. No event of consequence appears either in the ships journal or in our own private history till Friday the 19th of August when we discovered the island joanna – it is situated in 12 degrees south latitude: so that you may suppose we had there no occasion for stoves. The inhabitants find as little use either for clothes or beds – towns they have, and what they call houses, but as every house is a little hogstye so every town is a great one. We dined with one of the principal men of the place who called us his brethren, and treated us in a family way, that is, he gave us a very bad dinner and expected to be paid for it. This island is about 30 leagues in circumference, and is said to contain 30000 inhabitants, all black. The women shave their heads close, pill their ears down to their shoulders, and wear rings upon their noses. The men paint their teeth black and their nails red. Both sexes you see, in point of beauty, are almost as much indebted to art as they are to nature. In our dealings, we found them as well disposed to roguery as if they had had all the advantages of education after these strictures upon their morals, let us do justice to their religion. They profess to be Mahametans, but considering hoe scrupulous they are about ceremonies and how negligent of duties, one might easily mistake them for christians. In two days we had bullocks and poultry enough to stock a moderate farm, and took our leave of joanna, not a little edified by the observations we had made upon human nature in its primitive state of simplicity.

19th September 1774: The 28th of August we crossed the line a second time, and on the 15th of September found ourselves seriously in India. That day Ceylon presents itself to our view. The taphrobana of the ancients, the setrendil of the arabians, and Solomans magazine for spices, Ivory and Gold of Opher. Our first parents are supposed to have lived here in some splendour. After them, came Noah with his little family. In his time there was one just man at least upon the island, but things are much altered since the dutch took possession of it. On the 19th we got in sight of the coast of Coromandel.

21st September 1774: On the 21st saw the Flag Staff of Fort St George and prepared ourselves to lead a new life, at least for a day or two. There cannot be a more pleasing scene than the approach to Madras. But after such a voyage every shore has its charms. The coast though flat, is beautifully diversified with groves, forts, villages, and Pagodas. The Supreme Court of Judicature always take the lead. They arrived and landed two days before us. Scarce had we cast anchor when a letter and message arrived from the Governor, inviting us on shore. Several gentlemen of the council received us at the waters edge. The guns fired incessantly, the streets were lined with soldiers, the sun flamed in the zenith, the sand vitrified under our feet, the rabble trampled us to death. In short, we were received, like the fallen angels, into a little hell of our own. The governor entertained us at dinner each day. There was a concert the first evening, and afterward an Assembly and Supper. If splendour accompanied heat, a ball in India ought to be uncommonly splendid. The Ladies of Madras are more remarkable for their dancing than their beauty. The zeal and activity with which they except themselves is exercise enough for the spectators. By dint of motion, these Children of the Sun, in a very few minutes, get as hot as their father, and then it is not safe to approach them. In this agitation they continue, literally swimming through the dance, until he himself comes and reminds them of the hour – at midnight we sober citizens retired to bed.

22nd September 1774: Thursday morning, we mount a Phaeton and make an excursion for two hours. The place is very strongly fortified. We pass motes, draw bridges, gates and palisades without number. It would be well if the proprietors were half as secure from bankruptcy as their property is from insult. The villas about Madras are much in the style of those near rome, and, excepting the articles of pictures and natives not a whit less magnificent. The cultivated part of country is beautiful. In the gardens at least there reigns a verdure which we did not expect to find in so hot a climate and sandy a soil. Upon our return we passed through the black town, it was market day and even sort of jollity and noise going forward in the Bazar. The gentoos are divided into numberless classes or casts, distinguished from each other by marks or lines on the forehead, of different colours red, white, blue, yellow according to the degree of their faith or rank in the church. If philosophy consists in renouncing the comforts of life, there is not a black fellow here who might not give lessons to Diogenes, They are not robust, yet almost every man carries his fortune upon his back. The time of dining here seems unreasonable to a european but is perfectly calculated for the people of the country who have no idea of digestion, but in bed. A hearty dinner goes off insensibly in perspiration. After two hours sleep you waken with an appetite and are ready for your supper. The first and second day however, we had no time for indulgence. The Nabob of Arcot had sent various messages of civility to us, even before we landed, and it was agreed that we should pay him a visit in the evening. The avenue to his house was lined with horse and foot guards whose train of officers and servants attended at the steps, and conducted us into the Durbar or Hall of Audience, fitted up in the Asiatic manner with matts, sofas and cushions. Passing through this room to the stairfoot we found one of the Nabob's sons, who immediately embraced us. We next met with the same salutation from two others, planted upon the stairs, and lastly from the Nabob himself, who received us upon the first landing place. The ceremony over, he and his sons led us by hand into a large drawing room furnished after the European fashion. A conversation carried on through the channel of an interpreter cannot be very interesting; but it was very civil, and notwithstanding the ceremonies of asiatic politeness, the visit was too short to be tedious. When we had been seated a quarter of an hour, a train of servants came in with baskets and hails of gold. The Nabob then went round and presented each person with beelle, a kind of aromatic leaf which these people are everlastingly chewing, and dropped Otto of Roses upon our handkerchiefs. He then thanked everybody for the honour of their visit, and begged that an hour might be fixed for his returning it next day. Upon which, we took our leave, and retired in the order in which we came. I should have been very unwilling to have lost this interview with the Nabob, even such as it was, but it might have been rendered much more interesting. He might have shown us his women, or at least his elephants. He might, if the law had not put our virtue out of the reach of temptation, have presented each of us with a pearl, a Diamond, or a persian horse – such sweet remembrances make lasting impressions. I have now almost forgot the colour of His highnesses beard, it might be of the complexion of Hudibras's – some part of it at least was grey.

22nd September 1774 Continued: We supped at the Governor's in a large party, and next morning rode to St Thomas's mount, an almost perpendicular hill, ascended by long flights of hone steps – upon its summit there is a christian church. I do not insist that it stands upon the very spot where St Thomas suffered martyrdom, though the fact is generally believed, and boasted of by his votaries. Returning from the Apostle's shrine, we were shown a Banyan Tree, which not improperly might be called a Grove. It has been described a thousand times, yet I cannot help informing you that its branches descend till they touch the ground, where they take root and springing upwards become a new tree, that supports its parent. The progress of this wonderful tree is a perfect emblem of the true Principles of Colonisation. We next visited a curious manufacture of Chintz's, and after having been shown the whole process, from the loom to its glazing, returned to the Fort, time enough to dress and receive the Nabob's visit. His approach was announced by a royal salute upon his entering the Fort, I think I could more easily paint than describe the procession. A train of horse and foot-guards, a band of music, fellows with Gold and Silver staves, led horses, palanquins flaming with rich gold embroidery, the nabob was attended by his five sons and his elder brother, a venerable old man with a long white beard, who devotes his life to the study of retirement. They appeared in the same dress as yesterday, that is, in a long robe of fine white muslin and a turban of the same, without any ornament except a rich embroidered sash, in which is stuck a creese or differ. The complexion of this family are much fairer than that of the gentoos, but it is still a negative fairness, far, far distant from the happy blending of the lily with the rose in the faces of our companions. The Nabob after a short conversation, expressing a great desire to see them, a folding floor is opened at which the ladies stood, when he paid his complements to them in a very handsome manner. It was then proposed to walk to the . . . Company's arsenal a large and commodious building, containing 20000 hand of arms with artillery, stores of ammunition in abundance. The Nabob expressed great satisfaction, and upon our return embraced and took leave with a pompous speech full of professions of friendship and prayer for our success. In the evening, we embarked again in order to proceed to bengal.

22nd September 1774 Continued: For a few days, the events at Madras supplied us with new materials for conversation; but we soon reverted to the inspired system of a ship, and interesting dialogues upon the same topics, which have entertained us for the last six months.

6th October 1774: On Thursday the 6th of November [October] in the morning we weathered cape palominos and finding ourselves [torn] Ballasore road, concluded we were as good as at the end of our voyage. A multitude of congratulations were passed between the officers of the ship and the passengers when if we could have forseen what was to follow, we should rather have been employed in settling the state of the Consciences and in taking a final leave of each other. A pilot came on board us at noon.

7th October 1774: On Friday the 7th we weighed anchor, but made no progress.

8th October 1774: On the 8th repeated the same, with as little success.

9th October 1774: On Sunday the 9th got over the western brace in five fathom water, brought to and anchored in the kill – weighed again and got on the Eastern Brace in four fathom water, but the breeze failing, the ebb tide carried us back again – and while we were at Dinner, the ship struck twice. We then anchored in the Kill in four fathom water, and very near the breakers.

10th October 1774: Monday the 10th the Wind continuing

quite unfavourable, the pilot begun to be sensible of his finger, and saw the necessity of removing farther from the breakers. Still however we were at anchor between the braces, without anything to trust to, but the goodness [torn – unreadable]. Had it by stress of weather or any accident parted, we must inevitably have been lost, as there was not room enough to bring the ship up with another anchor. In the evening, there was every appearance of bad weather, and of the coming on us of a storm which never fails to attend at this season, the breaking up of the Monsoon. After Supper we entertained each other with minute and accurate accounts of the number of ships which had been lost or dismasted on such occasions – and in circumstances much less perilous than ours. This night it was observed that very little snoring was heard on board the ship – but a succession of doleful questions from the ignorant, with still more doleful answers from the Learned. We all wished ourselves once more in the open ocean.

11th October 1774: In the morning we resolved to call a council of the officers of the ship, to determine whether we should endeavour to ride out the storm, where we were, or return to Balladore Road, where, though we should have a little more room, in case the ship dragged or the cable parted, yet on the other hand, there was a heavier sea and worse anchorage. A person who [torn] circumstances, cannot conceive how difficult [torn] to decide in the Choice of Great Evils [torn] Death evidently depend upon the decision. [torn] resolved to stay where we were orders were given for lowering the top gallant masts a [torn] have [torn] anchored and cable ready to [torn] in case of accident. During the whole of this [torn] had nothing but violent squalls and rain.

12th October 1774: Wednesday the 12th The weather grew more moderate and the wind (inclined towards a favourable point).

13th October 1774: On Thursday the 13th at noon we attempted to weigh anchor, but were obliged, after much delay to cut our cable in order to save the tide. We at length passed the braces in safety which put a period to all our apprehensions. Braces are sand, shallows from the french word brasses.

14th October 1774: On the 14th in the afternoon our ship anchored in the mouth of the river, alongside the Men of War, where we found the Anson arrived two days before us. Sir Edward Hughes, who commanded the King's ships appointed to convey the councillors and Judges to Calcutta, reviewed them with all possible honours, and had made every disposition for [torn] ships and embarked in sloops and on budgerous in [torn] barges. After two days hurry and confusion [torn] removing our persons and baggage, we got under way; on Monday met a deputation from the governor and council in the river; Tuesday adjusted every article of the [torn] that night [torn] Fort William – and on Wednesday morning the 19th of October, made our public entry into Calcutta, and proceeded immediately to the Governor's House, where we dined.

2.6

Jane Bruce: Letter from Jane Bruce to Jamima Beck (1786)

Written several months after Jamima Beck had already died aboard the Rockingham, but before the news had reached the Bruces in India, this letter sheds light on the role and life of elite women in East India Company India. Jane Bruce had eloped with Craufurd Bruce to marry at Gretna Green only a year earlier, and was aged 17 or 18 at the time of writing. Hastily written to secure its place with an imminent dispatch of papers to Britain, the letter details the health of Jane Bruce and her infant son, Michael, as well as the social gossip of East India Company Bombay. This includes a list of marriages, ostracisation of older single women and accounts of the friendly relations between the Bruces and the Governor of Bombay. Jane Bruce would go on to have several other children with Craufurd, going on to live in Grosvenor Square with her increasingly wealthy husband, though ultimately would die in poverty following the bankruptcy of her husband in 1816.

My Dear Sister,

Having an Opportunity of writing you a few times over Land by a Despatch from Mr Scott's house, I have the pleasure to requent you that Mr Bruce & my little Michael are both very well, the latter we inoculated about a fortnight ago, and has had the small pox in the most favourable manner we could have wished for, his Beauty will not suffer in the least from them as the only one he had was on his back. I assure you I am very thankfull that it is over. I wish I could say I was well myself, the last time I wrote you I informed you, I was at the time very unwell with a fever which still continues &

comes on regularly every Spring. I have taken a great deal of Bark which appears to have very little effect, the Doctor is of opinion that it proceeds from Obstructions, & has therefore put me under a course of Mercury which I hope will put a stop to its Obstinacy.

Your Father & Mother will be happy to hear that their little Grandson has got the small pox over so ell I really wish they could see they would be highly pleased with him I am sure, for speaking impartially, he is without exception the finest Child I ever saw, he is not yet 4 months & a half old & can crawl a little, & sing a scotch tune to him, he can kick & fling as well as any Highlander; he is exceedingly good humoured for he scarcely even cries & to conclude the praises of my son I might not forget to tell you what the Widow says, says she if I thought I should have as lively a Boy as that, I would be married to marron. I believe she would be very happy to be married if she could get any offers to her liking.

Now that I am got on the subject of matrimony you will be very much surprised to hear of one that has taken place lately by a thing that no one expected to heare, Jovian took Boyce, they were married about 8 days ago & appear to be as much at their ease with each other, as if they had been married as many years – I had a long letter from Deliste the other Day he says he is preparing to go home in the month of December next he has been very much unwell with fever & liver Complaints, but was much better when he wrote. We have a great many marriages at present Sir Tores to Mrs Hatley, Dick Jones to the Elder Miss Ramsay, Mr Gate to Miss Mary Ramsay, Capt Don to Miss Rose, Mr Constable to Miss M Henny and the Widow to Colonel Degen, Poor Betsy Jurnen I am afraid will be autumn'd goods as no one wishes to take them off. Old Jenny Stark at last acknowledges herself to be old, she has entirely given up Dancing and very seldom goes out anywhere but she still continues friendly with her Battle – Our friend Dia is very well & is as happy as the day is long – Mr & Mrs Green are come down from Surat & our . . . does not blame herself a little on her Virginity, you know she never wanted that – his honnor is very well & still continues to be very attentive to Mr Bruce and myself we generally out with him twice a week & after he seldom forgets to Drink his friends that went home in the Rockingham.

If your sister is with you tell her I wish very much to commence a Correspondence with herself & that I am ashamed I have not wrote to her before but you know I am rather lazy, but mean to write to her the next opportunity.

I am only allowed to write on this scrap of paper so must defer saying any thing more till another Opportunity offers & you may be assured I won't fail in letting you hear from me.

When you route to Scotland be kind enough to remember me very particularly to all at Stenhouse & Brisbane & tell Mr Beck I am grown two inches since he saw me last – make my best love to him – & believe me to be yours most affectionately,

Jane Bruce

Mr Tullius: Journey to Aberdeen and Stonehaven (1824)

This short, light account of a trip to Aberdeenshire by Cupar lawyer and bachelor Mr Tullius provides a window into recreation among the professional classes in early nineteenth-century Scotland. Its detailed description of Dunnottar Castle is notable, both for the insights it gives around the castle's use and condition at the time and for Tullius's own conception of Scotland's history. Despite being written two centuries ago, almost all of the locations mentioned can still be visited, and in places the text flows as though it was written yesterday.

19th May 1824: Left Cupar at 3 o clock and arrived at the Commercial Line Pittenweem about 6. Called on Mr Cockburn B. P. and supped with him. Slept at the Inn.

20th May 1824: Breakfasted with Mr Cockburn and set sail with the Velocity Steamer for Aberdeen at 9 o clock, arrived at Aberdeen 6 o clock evening. Was much delighted by the accommodations of the vessel, and also with the appearance of the coast, which is the most part rocky and precipitous. Was prevented by the cold east wind from examining sufficiently the coast.

21st May 1824: Showery – went to see the Marshall College, but did not see the interior, the porter not being in the way – saw the King's College, and spent a considerable time in viewing the Library. Saw the Bridge of Don and was quite delighted by the appearance of the Don. The water is of a dark hue as it runs through moss. Saw the maiden hospital in which was an old woman with a very long white beard, which has made her very remarkable. Saw the Church of [blank] – the roof of which was covered with coats of arms beautifully coloured – was told that the Antiquarian Society had given £50 to an artist to take a copy of it. Saw for the first time a drag Goat with hassem geri in the canal. Viewed the Grey granite Quarry of which principally all the houses in and about Aberdeen, and which surpasses even Wheatstone in hardness. The Waterloo bridge in London was built of stone from this quarry. It is well worth going to see.

22nd May 1824: Viewed the Devanha Brewery – this is a very clean and effective Brewery and was originally built for a Paper Mill. They chiefly brew Porter and Some Strong Ale – Walked up the banks of the Dee, as far as the Bridge with 7 arches – crossed and proceeded to the coves, a small fishing village where Finnan Haddies are made, Dined in the Inn, ate them, and afterwards saw where and how they are made. The Dialect of the Fishers is curious and has a musical sound to my ear. This is likewise a station for preventative service. We returned to Aberdeen by the sea tide, and examined the needle, and bridge and the Downey hillock – which last is approximately so cold as the grass is quite soft – rested ourselves here, and saw the Velocity (steamer) pass quite close the needle. It is well worth visiting and is seen to most advantage when the tide is near to water. When close at the needle eye the rocks have a grand effect and from the entrance being even they brought to my recollection some of the descriptions which are given in the wonderful adventures of Lundbad bad the sailor – crossed the Dee in the ferryboat

23rd May 1824: Between sermons, walked along the shore, and returned by the sea coast.

24 May 1824: Was introduced by Mr James Duncan to Mr Wiley bookseller Mr Smith bookkeeper Mr Frost Dr and provost Brown doctor. Went accompanied with Mr and Mrs Duncan and Miss Dempster to see the lunatic asylum – which is kept in the greatest order, and every attention seems to be paid to the comfort and health of the patient – the number of patients was [blank].

25 May 1824: arrived at Stonehaven at nine per the velocity (Steamer) accompanied by Mr Duncan and Miss Dempster breakfasted at Collins mill Inn. Proceeded to view the ruins of the north of Castle – which stands upon a peninsula, about 3 miles south west from Stonehaven – the walk upon which the castle is built, and these in the neighbourhood are of a singular nature, being composed of small stones as if they were cemented, and from it resemblance to plum pudding, it has received the application of plum pudding rock. This place seems to have been of great strength, but from it being so completely commanded by the height, it never could not be rendered impregnable. In examining the castle we followed the directions of a guide, who is a rather old man who has plenty to see and he seems to delight in showing the castle. We entered by the door of the castle. This may seem to be superfluous, but routines are not always entered by the door where the portholes of the cannons are staring us in the face, and where six men were constantly standing century – we next came to the guardhouse, and hence to the interior of the castle. The guard here told us that the castle in all covered and enclosed 3 acres equals 15 Hallows as which where guaranteed for the soldiers, therefore which in the Square where they went through their exercises – the next led us into the commanding officers room whose chair is still standing which he was accustomed to set upon when viewing the manoeuvres of the soldiers which is in good view from another window of the same room he pointed out the garden of the burial-ground of the castle to the west. Below his shoulders seven chambers which were occupied with tradesmen of the seven different crafts. Nearby the centre of the castle is a large circular well which supplied the castle with water, it was 30 feet deep and about from 45 to 50 feet in circuit. He mentioned that treasure was said to have been held here but that a silver spoon and a gold coat of arms had only been found. He then showed us the Malthouse granary and kitchen, in which is still to be seen an astonishing large fireplace and two ovens and the next room stood the board to which the dishes were handed from the kitchen through the window and from which they were carried to table. He next showed us a place of confinement where the prisoners hands were fixed to the wall – they were fixed by means of wooden wedges and holes in the wall, which last are still visible. This is called (he said) the whig vault – he showed us next the black Hall or present, and mentioned a curious tradition concerning a spring of water – the prisoners were intended to be allowed to die with hunger, but in one night the water sprung through the rock and unchained them. There is a small hole towards the south through which nine effected their escape but were killed going down the precipice and were all buried in one grave in the castle burial-ground. Next the brewhouse, the gidys and the copper which was supplied with water by means of a pipe from the well – then the bakehouse, the oven of which is still remaining and then saw eight pieces of Canon. The one which was the furthest to the worst, he said was the largest and was called the Munch meg! And was so large that she dismantled a vessel at the small distance of 21 miles!! (The guide was not well pleased when one of her party did not seem inclined to believe this part of his testimony) he called the other seven the seven sisters. He then led us to the guardroom – to Lady Marshall's bedroom and dressing closet – to the hall – to the library – and to the Earls bedroom in which there is the coat of arms of him and his lady – the date of the arms is 1645 – he mentioned that the honourable Alex Keith intends to refit the room and put a roof upon it – to the dining room and Butlers pantry 50′ × 19′ to the drawing room and showed us the entry to the ballroom which was above the apartment occupied by the seven craft – and is 120 feet long but above the chamber there is a bedroom. Then he went upstairs to the bedroom 'were two years ago Lord Aldershot and a party took a luncheon'

(language of guide). Then he went to the chapel where he said
that Sir William Wallace burnt 5000 men – but this number
must have been much exaggerated, as from the appearance
of the place I do not think that it could hold so many men.
The mark of the pulpit is still seen and the stones for holding
the holy water. He next showed us Waterton Lodge, which
is on the right hand as you enter the castle and which is said
to have been the first built house of the castle. To the left of
which is the stables and he laughed and at the south end of
which were some dwelling houses for soldiers – further to the
north and east was a Smith's shop and further north still was
the baths and kitchens and to the south is to sellers for the use
of the D kitchens. There is a hole in the pantry of the kitchen
which was made for holding the crown, the sword and the
sceptre. Above is the tower from the top of which was the
watchtower of the castle. The view from this is grand, a fine
expanse of sea, and the neighbouring Cape and the rugged
cliffs of rocks give it a grand and interesting appearance. The
siege of the Watchman is 250 feet above the level of the sea,
our guide told us that a few years ago when showing the castle
to a party she having spotted the lock of the door could not
shut and when he returned with a Smith from Stonehaven
and locked the door, he locked in a poor woman who had
been gathering Dolce, and who had entered unperceived in
his absence and the woman not having observed him locking
the door could not get out so she was obliged to pass the night
in durance vile amongst the ruins. He showed us the bed she
made for herself with new cut hay – she was obliged to remain
in from 1 o clock the one day until 4 o clock the other. He
next showed us the window by which Sir William Wallace
entered when he took the castle and on which account it has
received the appellation of the Wallace window – next the
powder magazine. It may be necessary to mention that the
Governor of the Castle Captain John Hay keeps a register in
which are to be found the names of most of the visitors who
have honoured the castle with their presence. We observed
among it the name of Mr Kean from the Theatre Royal Drury

Lane. After our return to Stonehaven, we took a walk up the road to Dunnottar house which was most delightful. We dined in Collins and returned to Aberdeen per the Bulliant Steamer, much delighted with our days jaunt. I may mention that the day was most delightful. (Was introduced to Mr B. S. Stonehaven)

26th May 1824: Went and examined the Marshall College and was delighted to see that the museum was kept in most excellent condition, and that the minerals, coins etc are not as in St Andrews in the greatest confusion, but kept in glass cases and arranged in the greatest regularity. The instruments of the Natural Philosophy class even, are [end of material].

Appendix 1

Timeline of Key Events

1323	Creation of earliest documentation still held by firm, copy of charter of Robert the Bruce
1529	Papal Bull of Clement VII seeking to quell Reformation in Scotland
1631	Death of Cuthbert Miller, first verifiable predecessor to present-day firm by master–apprentice lineage
1693	Thomas Pringle, the first predecessor to become Deputy Keeper of the Signet, is admitted as a WS
1701	John Lumsden, founder of what would become Bruce & Kerr, admitted as a WS
1712	Alexander Stevenson of Montgreenan, first common link between J&F Anderson, Strathern & Blair and Bell & Scott, admitted as a WS
1749	John Davidson admitted as a WS, shortly after establishing practice
1770	John Davidson begins work for Duke of Buccleuch following involvement in Douglas Cause
1770–96	Alexander Duncan manages affairs of Beck and Bruce families, and secures legitimisation for Charlotte Stewart
1793	Thomas Cranstoun establishes office at 48 Castle Street in the Edinburgh New Town
1819	John Gibson, solicitor for Sir Walter Scott, admitted a WS
1826–32	John Gibson manages a trust designed to rescue Sir Walter Scott from bankruptcy

1842   John Gibson opens Granton Harbour on behalf of the Duke of Buccleuch

1880–83   John Inglis writes a diary during his time as clerk at J&F Anderson

1888   Robert Strathern secures environmental protection for the River Esk

1901–2   Alexander Stevenson Blair assists Mrs De Falbre with investigations for her divorce

1914–18   Various members of historical practices participate in the First World War

1935   Arthur Russell helps secure parts of Glencoe for the National Trust for Scotland

1939–45   Various members of historical practices participate in the Second World War

1940   Margaret Maud Mitchell becomes the first female solicitor, and later partner, at J&F Anderson

1943   Ian Drummond Mackenzie is killed in action in Tunisia

1974   Expansion to Haddington with offices specialising in property

1982–3   Computerisation of offices of J&F Anderson and Strathern & Blair

1992   J&F Anderson and Strathern & Blair merge to form Anderson Strathern

1999   Publication of Pocket Canon Bibles through the Bible Board

2004   Move from Castle Street and Charlotte Street to Rutland Court

2005   Anderson Strathern expands to Glasgow, with first offices on Hope Street

2011   Anderson Strathern merges with Bell & Scott

2021   Expansion to Kilmarnock at the Halo Centre and opening of Shetland office

Appendix 2

Historical Practices

Partners are shown in bold.

J&F ANDERSON to 1900

Cuthbert Miller (WS c. 1585, d. 1631)
⅄
John Bayne (WS 1655, d. 1681) (Apprentice to Cuthbert Miller)
⅄
John MacFarlane (WS 1678, d. 1709) (Treasurer of the Signet, Apprentice to John Bayne)
⅄
Thomas Pringle (WS 1693, d. 1736) (Deputy keeper of the Signet, apprentice to John McFarlane)
⅄
Alexander Stevenson of Montgreenan (WS 1712, d. 1755) (Apprentice to Thomas Pringle)
⅄
Samuel Mitchelson (WS 1736, d. 1788) (Apprentice to Alexander Stevenson)
⅄
Thomas Cranstoun (WS 1786, d. 1836) (Apprentice to Samuel Mitchelson)
⅄
George Veitch (WS 1809, d. 1826) (Apprentice to Thomas Cranstoun)
⅄
John Anderson (WS 1824, d. 1864) (Apprentice to Thomas Cranstoun, son of John Anderson WS of historical branch)
⅄
Thomas Trotter-Cranstoun (WS 1823, d. 1848) (Apprentice to William Bell and nephew of Thomas Cranstoun)
⅄
Francis Anderson (WS 1837, d. 1855) (Apprentice to Thomas Cranstoun, nephew of John Anderson)
⅄
Alexander Wood (WS 1850, d. 1852) (Apprentice to Thomas Trotter-Cranstoun)
⅄
Frederick Pitman (WS 1857, d. 1896) (Apprentice to John Anderson, nephew of John Anderson)
⅄
John Ramsay Anderson (WS 1874, d. 1926) (Apprentice to Frederick Pitman, son of Francis Anderson)
⅄
William Hugh Murray (WS 1872, d. 1921) (Apprentice to Frederick Pitman, no relation)
⅄
Allan Bertram MacAllan (WS 1858, d. 1888) (Apprentice to David Smith – not in firm, no relation)
⅄
Archibald Robert Craufurd Pitman (WS 1881, d. 1924) (Apprentice to and son of Frederick Pitman)
⅄
John MacLachlan (WS 1885, d. 1941) (Apprentice to Frederick Pitman, no relation)

STRATHERN & BLAIR to 1900

Cuthbert Miller (WS c. 1585, d. 1631)

∀

John Bayne (WS 1655, d. 1681) (Apprentice to Cuthbert Miller)

∀

John MacFarlane (WS 1678, d. 1709) (Treasurer of the Signet, Apprentice to John Bayne)

∀

Thomas Pringle (WS 1693, d. 1736) (Deputy Keeper of the Signet,
apprentice to John McFarlane)

∀

Alexander Stevenson of Montgreenan (WS 1712, d. 1755) (Apprentice to Thomas Pringle)

∀

George Balfour (WS 1736, d. 1751) (Apprentice to Alexander Stevenson,
son-in-law of Alexander Stevenson)

∀

John Davidson of Stewartfield and Haltree (WS 1749, d. 1797)
(Deputy Keeper of the Signet, Apprentice to George Balfour)

∀

John Home (WS 1812 but practised long before, d. 1831) (Apprentice to Davidson)

∀

Hay Donaldson (WS 1802, d. 1822) (Apprentice to John Moir)

∀

John Gibson (WS 1819, d. 1877) (Apprentice to James Nairne)

∀

William Home (WS 1823, d. 1846) (Apprentice to and son of John Home)

∀

Henry Gordon Gibson (WS 1851, d. 1869) (Apprentice to and son of John Gibson)

∀

John Home (WS 1866, d. 1890) (Apprentice to John Gibson and Henry Gordon Gibson,
Grandson of John Home)

∀

Robert Strathern (WS 1872, d. 1921) (Apprentice to John Gibson and
Henry Gordon Gibson)

∀

John Henry Gibson (WS 1888, d. 1898) (Apprentice to Robert Strathern,
son of Henry Gordon Gibson)

∀

Alexander Stevenson Blair (WS 1889, d. 1936) (Apprentice to Wright and Blyth)

∀

Charles James Penn (WS 1891, d. 1930) (Apprentice to and brother-in law of
Robert Strathern)

BELL & SCOTT

Cuthbert Miller (WS c. 1585, d. 1631)
∀

John Bayne (WS 1655, d. 1681) (Apprentice to Cuthbert Miller)
∀

John MacFarlane (WS 1678, d. 1709) (Treasurer of the Signet, Apprentice to John Bayne)
∀

Thomas Pringle (WS 1693, d. 1736) (Deputy Keeper of the Signet, apprentice to John McFarlane)
∀

Alexander Stevenson of Montgreenan (WS 1712, d. 1755) (Apprentice to Thomas Pringle)
∀

George Balfour (WS 1736, d. 1751) (Apprentice to Alexander Stevenson, son-in-law of Alexander Stevenson)
∀

John Davidson of Stewartfield and Haltree (WS 1749, d. 1797) (Apprentice to George Balfour)
∀

Hugh Corrie (WS 1772, d. 1805) (Apprentice to John Davidson)
∀

William Bell (WS 1807, d. 1849) (Apprentice to Hugh Corrie)
∀

Benjamin William Bell (WS 1833, d. 1840) (Apprentice to and son of William Bell)
∀

Robert Craigie Bell (WS 1864, d. 1912) (Apprentice to Mackenzie & Ballie, son of Benjamin Bell)
∀

Stuart Neilson (WS 1850, d. 1886) (Apprentice to John Irving)
∀

John Scott (WS 1885, d. 1944) (Apprentice to R. C. Bell)
∀

Benjamin Bell (WS 1898, d. 1932) (Apprentice to J. Mylne, son of R. C. Bell)
∀

John Hay Smith (WS 1930, d. 1961) (Apprentice to John Scott)
∀

James Gibson (b. 1860, d. 1939) (SSC, father-in-law of John Hay Smith)
∀

Archibald Henderson Elder (WS 1936, retired 1978) (uncertain of apprenticeship)
∀

James Ian Hay Smith (WS 1952) (son of John Hay Smith)

BRUCE & KERR to 1900

John Mudie (Born before 1600, d. 1648)

Robert Alexander (WS 1638, d. 1667) (Apprentice to John Mudie)
∀

William Thomson (WS 1661, d. 1693) (Apprentice to Robert Alexander)
∀

William Thomson (WS 1681, d. 1708) (Apprentice to his father William Thomson)
∀

John Lumsden of Blanerne (WS 1701, d. 1757) (Apprentice to William Thomson, grandson of General Robert Lumsden)
∀

James Graham of Damside (WS 1731, d. 1763) (Apprentice to John Lumsden, nephew of John Lumsden and uncle of James Beck)
∀

Alexander Duncan (WS 1765, d. 1821) (Apprentice to James Graham, his uncle-in-law)
∀

John Yule (WS 1818, d. 1851) (Apprentice to Alexander Duncan)
∀

William Stevenson (WS 1810, d. ?) (Apprentice to Alexander Duncan, his nephew)
∀

Alexander Bruce SSC. (b. 1799, d. 1872) (Apprentice to cousin Thomas Ferguson)
∀

James Bruce (WS unknown, b. 1838, d. 1915) (Apprentice and nephew of Alexander Bruce)
∀

James Renton SSC (Uncertain apprenticeship)
∀

Thomas Kerr (b. 1843, d. 1916) (Uncertain apprenticeship)
∀

Merged with Bell & Scott 1964

Appendix 3

Recent History of Anderson Strathern

Upon moving from the New Town offices to Rutland Court in 2004, Anderson Strathern experienced an acceleration in change. The expansion and modernisation that the new premises facilitated brought in a flood of talent, with a considerable diversification of social, cultural and economic backgrounds. Significantly, the partnership of the firm was for the first time composed mainly of men and women with a state education. In the J&F Anderson branch of the firm, it is likely that Douglas Stewart, who joined the firm in 1955 and became a partner in 1961, was the first partner to come from such a background. The current board of the firm has an equal, though unenforced, gender split, with the overall partnership having among the highest proportion of women of any independent Scottish law firm. Nevertheless, while access has improved, there are still lengths to go, with a 2019 survey finding only 2% of female lawyers feel there is equality between genders within the profession.

In 2005 the firm decided to move beyond the traditional confines of Edinburgh and become established in Scotland's commercial capital – Glasgow. Work had been done in Glasgow in much earlier times, including James Graham's involvement as a solicitor there. Expansion to Glasgow had also been explored by J&F Anderson in the 1980s, but in the end was not put into practice. This status quo eventually changed when a group of Anderson Strathern solicitors established a small office on Glasgow's Buchanan Street, later expanding to Blythswood Square following the acquisition of the commercial solicitors Kerr & Co.

In less than a decade, this small satellite office had snowballed into an extensive office on George Square, with a quarter of the total business operating from that building. With Glasgow home to the busiest civil court not only in Scotland, but in all of Europe, there was ample room for future expansion. Today, Glasgow forms one of what former Chairman Robert Carr described as the 'twin pillars' of Anderson Strathern, alongside Edinburgh.

In seeking to offer a service across Scotland, Anderson Strathern has increasingly taken on the legal work of public authorities from local councils to the Scottish Government, as well as educational institutions such as Ayrshire College, the University of St Andrews and Glasgow Caledonian University. The tradition of supporting new technologies and industries also continues. Just as John Gibson helped bring about the first railroads and steam docks in Edinburgh, and Douglas Stewart worked with those involved in the extraction of North Sea oil, so today work is being done with an organisation that is sending rockets into space from a new facility on Shetland, where Anderson Strathern opened an office in 2021.

Beyond Scotland, Anderson Strathern has become an integral part of the Association of European Lawyers, which it helped found as Strathern & Blair in 1988. The association, which includes members from Reykjavik to Moscow, collaborates on complex cross-border transactions which have become more relevant with the increased standardisation of law, both inside and outside the European Union, and also with the renewed importance of international collaboration in general. As the only Scottish firm in the association, and one of only five British firms included, Anderson Strathern holds sole responsibility for bringing Scotland's unique legal system into the mix, ensuring that Scottish businesses and services are given due consideration across Europe. With Britain's exit from the European Union, this has become an even more vital link between Scotland and the rest of Europe as many other roads of cooperation are closed.

Following in the tradition of Robert Strathern's pioneering work on environmental pollution, Anderson Strathern has recently been highly commended in the Climate Change and Sustainability category of the Financial Times' Innovative Lawyers Report. Most notably, Anderson Strathern was recognised for working with the

Crown Estate to develop the world's first renewable marine energy-generation plant in the Pentland Firth. Such accolades have contributed towards a ranking in the Chambers legal directory in the 'Professional Discipline – Best of the UK' category, making Anderson Strathern the only Scottish firm to achieve such a ranking.

The company was also awarded the 2019 award for 'Firm of the Year – Scottish Independents' and 'Employment Team of the Year' at the Herald Law Awards. The judges commended the company's attention to financial management and commitment to staff well-being in particular. An example of this is a longstanding commitment to the Investors in People campaign. Having been part of the scheme for over ten years, Anderson Strathern stands as the longest running participant in the scheme of any law firm.

Anderson Strathern has now established a presence in Kilmarnock, Ayrshire. With the aim of offering a local service drawing on the talents of the national firm, the new office is based at the HALO Centre on the grounds of the former Johnnie Walker plant in the heart of the town. Alexander Stevenson, the solicitor upon which the historical branches of Anderson Strathern converge, was born only a few miles away, making this as much a homecoming as the breaking of new ground.

Select Bibliography

Anderson Strathern Sources

The materials enumerated below were uncovered in several boxes and in two iron chests at Anderson Strathern's Rutland Court office between 2018 and 2019. Several years earlier, a separate iron chest was opened and its contents were deposited with the NRS. The documents and items discovered at Anderson Strathern have been listed in the order and groupings in which they were originally discovered.

1. MacPherson Family Tree (unknown)
2. Bell and Scott Timeline (1794–1964)
3. Articles of Settlement on Marriage of Richard Syme and Suzanna Gilbert (1772)
4. Instrument of Assignation (1725)
5. Articles of Settlement on Marriage of R. J. Hebdon and C. H. Walker (1839)
6. Deeds of Distribution to Creditors of A. Lindberg (1730)
7. Deeds Relating to Isabella Murray, Lord and Lady Hillbank, Viscount Dundee and 'An Opinion from an Advocate' (1780–1836)
8. Household Account of Alexander Duncan (c. 1800)
9. Statements of Income Tax (1847–50)
10. Correspondence from India P. C. Bruce to J. Beck (1788)
11. Several Metal Shoe Buckles (unknown)
12. Leatherbound Bible Designated as a Wedding Gift (1698)
13. The Governance of the Church of Scotland by Rev. J. Brown of Haddington (1767)

14. Notes on Family Lineage Compiled by Robert Lumsden of Strathvithie (unknown)
15. Letters of Legitimisation in Favour of Charlotte Stewart and Privy Seal of Scotland (1796)
16. Edition of the Straits Times Extra (1856)
17. List of Wines Sold by Cockburns and Campbell and General Belfour's Wine Account (1834–5)
18. Inquiry into an Unknown Woman's Health from M. E. Bowes Strathmore (1785)
19. Grant of Patronage by Lord Gray to Andrew Morton in Scots (1529)
20. Guide to the Coronation of Queen Victoria (1838)
21. Invitations and Tickets to the Coronation of William IV (1830)
22. Copy of Act of Parliament Revoking All Acts and Charters post–1639 (1662)
23. Commission of J. R. Bruce as Major (1914)
24. Commission of James Bruce as Second Lieutenant (1901)
25. Letters from India During the Rebellion (1857)
26. Accounts of Expenses of Churches in Ireland (1827)
27. Report from Begging Letters Department with Signature of Marquess of Bute (1846)
28. Invitation from Lady Moira to Mrs French to a Charity Fancy Dress Ball (1830)
29. Gossip Column Concerning an Appeal by William Ralston to General Assembly (1765)
30. Accounts of Visits Concerning the Mental Health of Sir Thomas Moncrieffe by Duncan (1796–8)
31. Lock of Hair of Lady Sophia Hastings (c. 1830)
32. Recipe for Eye Drops (unknown)
33. Receipt for School Fees from Headmaster of Errol (1735)
34. Caledonian Mercury Newspaper (1843)
35. Investor Advice Book of A. J. Wilson (1893)
36. Letters from Madras and Hyderabad (1814–34)
37. Northwest Iowa Promotion Document (c. 1880)
38. Course of Study and Fees for the Merchant Maiden Hospital (1858)

39. State of Funds Belonging to Duncan's Trustees (c. 1821)
40. Pamphlet Documenting Scottish Legal Life (1899)
41. Documents Relating to Thistle Court Offices in Edinburgh (1855)
42. Tack Between J. Morrias and A. Garden (1701)
43. Diary of Journey to India and Letters Between P. C. Bruce and J. Beck (1774)
44. Letters of P. C. Bruce and J. Beck Often Addressed to Coffee Houses (c. 1780)
45. Account of War in India from G. Simpson Discussing Troop Numbers and Indian Politics (1791)
46. Trustees' Minutes Regarding Sale of RBS Stock by Auction (1802)
47. Bank of Scotland Notice of Rights to Issue Shares (1829)
48. Draft Letter from Duncan Declining to Act for a Client (1816)
49. Petition by Duncan for Restoration of a Pew (1819)
50. Copy of Feu Charter and a Heritable Bond (1482, 1505)
51. Report on Sabbath Profanation (1834)
52. Regulations for Mrs Trotter's Girls School (1843)
53. Lampoon on 'Muir's Death' (c. 1700–1900)
54. Memorial to the Banished After Battle of Sandwich in Upper Canada by J. M. Aitchison (1839)
55. Journey to Middleton (1817)
56. Patrick Crauford Family Tree (1964)
57. Lady Duncan's Tax Bill (1827)
58. Account Books of A. Thomson (1830–3)
59. Letters Between Brash and Mackenzie (1834–1836)
60. Sealed Document with George IV's Signature Mentioning Dundas, Acceptance of John MacKinley to Become a Burgess of Rothesay and Document Regarding Bute Militia (1809–1821)
61. Sasines by Gilbert McConqufry and Separate Sasine (1557, 1618)
62. Various Instruments of Sasines (1600–1800)
63. Obituary of J. Bruce in *The Scotsman* (1915)
64. Duncan Family Tree (1964)
65. Table of Fees Payable to Town Clerk (1790)
66. Act of Land Reclamation and Drainage at River Leven, Fife (1827)

67. Report on Repairs Required to Various Roads and Bridges in Fife (1725)
68. Indenture (1821)
69. Commission as a WS (1827)
70. Habeus Corpus Acts (1752)
71. Copies of Letters Regarding Defects of 1701 Act for Preventing Wrongful Imprisonment of Civilians (1752)
72. Bulletin on Illness of George IV (1830)
73. Notes on Debates That Took Place in the Commons (1752)
74. Bill to Amend 1701 Act (1735)
75. Bill to Amend 1701 Act (1752)
76. Selection of Short Fictional Writings by James Beck (1770)
77. Letter from Bruce to Ms C. Thomson (1837)
78. Scale of Distribution of Booty in Pindaree and Maharatta War (1828)
79. Invitation to Dinner from Mendelssohn to Sir A. Johnston (1829)
80. Nagpur and Berar Times (1913)
81. Expenditure Account of Tour From Edinburgh to Fort William (1870)
82. Rate Receipt (1819)
83. Receipt for 'The Park' (1761)
84. Receipt for Hair Powder Duty (1796)
85. Catalogue of Alexander Duncan's Library (1794)
86. Letter From F. Ronaldson to His Niece on Her Marriage (1807)
87. Renunciation of John McAngus in Favour of Gilbert McConqufry (1588)
88. The following documents appear as part of a bundle:
    i. Dispensation and Assignation from Walter Scott to Mrs Scott (1769)
    ii. Rights to Rev. to Farm Two Cows on a Farm from Alex Campbell (1786)
    iii. Charge Against Two Soldiers by Lord Auchinleck (1768)
    iv. Tutorial Inventory of Robert Whyte with the Architect John Adam's Signature (1766)
    v. Indenture Between Coutts and Muirhead (1762)
    vi. Deed of Jailzie by Couttz (1759)

vii.   Letter Appointing Quartermaster during the Battle of Prestonpans by the Earl of Stair (1745)

viii. Letter for Inspection of Jacobite Man of War Following Culloden (1746)

ix.   Jacobite Letter (1746)

x.   Receipt of Funds from the Earl of Loudoun (1726)

xi.   Receipt for Membership of New Club for John Balfour (1835)

xii.   Letter on Requirement to Reform the Highlands (1725)

xiii. Copy of a Letter by James Anderson on Receiving Gifts Following Marion Pringle Being Condemned to Death for Adultery (1694)

xiv.   Letter From Lord Panmure Confirming a Severe Reduction to the Inheritance of His Daughters for Their Disobedience (c. 1830)

xv.   Letter from the Earl of Conway at the Court of Charles II Discussing the Return of the Duke of York to Court (1681)

xvi.   Letter for O'Neil from Joseph Wilkins (unknown date)

89.   Letter from Bombay (1788)

90.   Seal of King George III (c. 1790)

91.   Ink Well Stopper (unknown date)

92.   Patrick Lindsay Will and Translation (1671)

93.   Disposition and Assignation by Adam Smith (1754)

94.   Document by William Milne (1715)

95.   A bundle of curiosities belonging to Mr Gibson, which notably includes:

   i.   Receipts for New Clothes and Stationery After University (c. 1810)

   ii.   Book on Playing the Flute and Receipt for Learning (1822)

   iii. Letter from Mr Gibson Regarding a Visit by Queen Victoria to the Duke of Buccleuch (undated)

96.   An Additional Bundle of Curiosities Belonging to Mr Gibson (c. 1810–1860)

97.   Old Photographs of J&F Anderson, Apprentice and Partnerships Lists, 1985 Views on Future, (c. 1950–1992)

98. Documents Concerning Previous NRS Donations of Strathern & Blair (1979)
99. Partnership Meetings' Minutes for J&F Anderson (c. 1980)
100. Ledgers of Strathern & Blair (1919–23)
101. Bankruptcy Case (1896–8)
102. Caldwell Case (c. 1899)
103. Miscellaneous Documents (c. 1880–1920)
104. Notes on Writing Lawful Union, Pamphlet by J&F Anderson 1985, Book About the Battle of Britain (1940–98)
105. Collection of Seven Books, Including Letter Books Belonging to Alexander Stevenson Blair (1880–1920)

Primary Sources

British Library, London. IOR/L/MAR/B/124-I(1), Captain John Blanshard, Rockingham: Ledger (1786–1787).

British Library, London. IOR/L/MAR/B/124A, Captain John Blanshard, Rockingham: Journal (1786–1787).

Edinburgh Commissary Court, CC8/8/119, James Graham Will and Testament (6/4/1764).

Edinburgh Commissary Court, CC8/8/127, James Thomas Bruce Will and Testament (2/1/1788).

National Archives, London. PROB11/1162, James Beck, Will of James Beck (15/3/1788).

National Archives, London. PROB 31/786/282, Estate of Patrick Craufurd Bruce, of Bombay in the East Indies (1789).

NLS, MS. 3417, Correspondence of Allan Ramsay, the painter, and John Davidson, Writer to the Signet, about their dispute over property at Ramsay Garden, Edinburgh (1757–60).NLS, MS. 8297, Correspondence of Andrew Stuart with John Davidson, Writer to the Signet, Antiquary (1787–97).

NLS, MSS.16755–16759, Legal correspondence, chiefly of the Edinburgh lawyers of the Fletcher family, John Davidson, Writer to the Signet (1766–80), his partner Hugh Warrender, Writer to the Signet (1777–1806), and Gibson and Fraser, Writers to the Signet (1851–4), with the family and other lawyers (1766–1854).

NLS, MS. 10787, Letter book of John Davidson of Stewartfield,

Writer to the Signet, containing correspondence with his clients on their estate and financial business (1774–7).

NLS, MS. 14835, Letter of John Home, author of 'Douglas', to John Home at John Davidson's, Castle Hill, Edinburgh, concerning family and personal matters (21 July 1793)

NLS, MS. 29.5.8(iv), Letters of, among others, William Robertson (undated), William Ogilvie (1774–79), John Davidson (1770–89 and undated), the Earl of Buchan (1780–1804 and undated), Francis Grose (1789 and undated), John Nichols (1781–5) and George Chalmers (1792–1800).

NRS, Census 453/6/13, Robert Pattullo (1841).

NRS, Census 685/2/23, Jamima Beck (1851).

NRS, GD214/726, Duchess of Hamilton to John Davidson (c. 1776).

NRS, GD224/930/32, Davidson's Correspondence (c. 1760–80).

NRS, GD240/18/4, James Beck, Receipts of James Beck (c. 1777).

NRS, GD240/30/6, James Beck and Jamima Bruce, Personal Correspondence (1786–1787).

NRS, GD240/41/5, James Beck, Will of James Beck (1777).

NRS, Old Parish Registers of Birth 485/10204 Larbert, James Thomas Bruce (24/3/1758).

St Andrews, SC, msdep76/11/1, James Cheape, Inventory of James Beck (8/2/1790).

Secondary Sources

Abir-Am, Pnina, *Uneasy Careers and Intimate Lives: Women in Science, 1789–1979* (New Brunswick, 1987).

Armitage, David, *The Ideological Origins of the British Empire* (Cambridge, 2000).

Armitage, David, 'Empire and Liberty: A Republican Dilemma' in *Republicanism: A Shared European Heritage* (Cambridge, 2002), pp. 29–46.

Ashplant, T. G. and Wilson, Adrian, 'Whig History and Present-centred History', *Historical Journal*, vol. 31, no. 1 (1988), pp. 1–16.

Barrow, Geoffrey (ed.), *The Declaration of Arbroath: History, Significance, Setting* (Edinburgh, 2003).

Brake, Laurel, Kaul, Chandrika and Turner, Mark W. (eds), *The News of the World and the British Press, 1843–2011: 'Journalism for the Rich, Journalism for the Poor'* (London, 2015)

Brown, Iain Gordon, 'Allan Ramsay's Rise and Reputation', *Volume of the Walpole Society*, vol. 50 (1984), pp. 209–47.

Brown, Iain Gordon, *Abbotsford and Sir Walter Scott: The Image and the Influence* (Edinburgh, 2003).

Brown, K. M., *The Records of the Parliaments of Scotland to 1707* (St Andrews, 2015).

Bowen, Hugh, *Revenue and Reform: The Indian Problem in British Politics, 1757–1773* (Cambridge, 1991).

Bowen, Hugh, *The Business of Empire: The East India Company and Imperial Britain, 1756–1833* (Cambridge, 2007).

Bowen, H. W., Lincoln, Margarette and Rigby, Nigel (eds), *The Worlds of the East India Company* (Woodbridge, 2002).

Bowler, Peter, *Evolution: The History of an Idea*, 3rd edn (Berkeley, CA, 2003).

Bruce, Ian, *The Nun of Lebanon* (London, 1951).

Butterfield, Herbert, *The Whig Interpretation of History* (London, 1931).

Cairns, John, 'The Law, the Advocates and the Universities in Late Sixteenth-Century Scotland', *Scottish Historical Review*, vol. 73, no. 193 (1994), pp. 171–90.

Cairns, John, 'Advocates' Hats, Roman Law and Admission to the Scots Bar, 1580–1812', *Journal of Legal History*, vol. 20 (1999), pp. 24–61.

Cairns, John, 'The Legal Education of Alexander Mylne, First President of the College of Justice', in *De Rubus Divinis et Humanis* (Gottingen, 2009), pp. 15–24.

Cannon, John, *The Fox–North Coalition: Crisis of the Constitution, 1782–4* (New York, 1969).

Carlyle, Thomas, *On Heroes, Hero-Worship, and the Heroic in History* (London, 1841).

Colley, Linda, 'Multiple Kingdoms', *London Review of Books*, vol. 23, no. 14 (2001), pp. 23–4.

Davis, Natalie Zemon, *The Return of Martin Guerre* (Princeton, NJ, 1983).

Dawson, Jane, *Scotland Reformed 1488–1587* (Edinburgh, 2007).

Debrett, John, *A Correct List of Knights, Citizens and Burgesses Elected to Serve in the Parliament Appointed to Meet at Westminster on Tuesday* (London, 1802).

Decisions of the Court of Session, J. Anderson and Company (Edinburgh, 1831).

Devine, T. M., *The Tobacco Lords: A Study of the Tobacco Merchants of Glasgow and their Trading Activities, c. 1740–90* (Edinburgh, 1975).

Devine, T. M. (ed.), *Recovering Scotland's Slavery Past: The Caribbean Connection* (Edinburgh, 2015).

Devine, T. M., *Independence or Union: Scotland's Past and Scotland's Present* (London, 2017).

Devine, Tom and McCarthy, A. (eds), *The Scottish Experience in Asia, c. 1700 to the Present* (Edinburgh, 2016).

Dickens, A. G., *The English Reformation* (London, 1964).

Dickson, J. W., Dunbar, W. H. and Rymer, John, *The Scottish Jurist, Containing Reports of Cases Decided in the House of Lords, Courts of Session, Teinds, and Exchequer, and the Jury and Justiciary Courts,* Vol. III (Edinburgh, 1830).

Dray, William, 'J. H. Hexter, Neo-Whiggism and Early Stuart Historiography', *History and Theory,* vol. 26, no. 2 (1987), pp. 133–49.

Dunbar, John G., *Scottish Royal Palaces: The Architecture of the Royal Residences during the Late Medieval and Early Renaissance Periods* (Edinburgh, 1999).

Eaton, Natasha, 'The Art of Colonial Despotism: Portraits, Politics and Empire', *Cultural Critique,* no. 70 (2008), pp. 63–93.

The Edinburgh Almanack, Or Universal Scots and Imperial Register (Edinburgh, 1828).

Fairburn, Miles, *Social History: Problems, Strategies and Methods* (London, 1999).

Finn, Margot, 'The Female World of Love and Empire: Women, Family & East India Company Politics at the End of the Eighteenth Century', *Gender and History,* vol. 31 (2019), pp. 7–24.

Finn, Margot and Smith, Kate (eds), *The East India Company at Home 1757–1857* (London, 2018).

Fisher, Michael, 'Representations of India, the English East India

Company, and Self by an Eighteenth-Century Indian Emigrant to Britain', *Modern Asian Studies*, vol. 32, no. 4 (1998), pp. 891–911.

Foote, Sam, *The Nabob* (London, 1772).

Forbes, James, *Oriental Memoirs*, Vol. 4 (London, 1813).

Forrest, George W., *Selections from the Letters Dispatches and Other State Papers* (Bombay, 1888).

Forsyth, D. and Ugolini, W. (eds), *A Global Force: War, Identities and Scotland's Diaspora* (Edinburgh, 2016).

Foxon, David, *Libertine Literature in England, 1660–1745* (London, 1965).

George Buchanan, *De Iure Regni apud Scotos Dialogus* (Edinburgh, 1579).

Gibson, John, *Reminiscences on Sir Walter Scott* (Edinburgh, 1871).

Gillespie, Robert, *Round about Falkirk* (Glasgow, 1879).

Ginzburg, Carlo, *The Cheese and the Worms* (Baltimore, MD, 1980).

Glass, Bryan and Mackenzie, John (eds), *Scotland, Empire and Decolonisation in the Twentieth Century* (Manchester, 2015).

Haigh, Christopher, *English Reformations: Religion, Politics and Society under the Tudors* (Oxford, 1975).

Hall, A., 'On Whiggism', *History of Science*, vol. 21, no. 1 (1983), pp. 45–59.

Harrison, J. G., *Rebirth of a Palace: The Royal Court at Stirling Castle* (Edinburgh, 2011).

Hexter, J. H., *Reappraisals in History: New Views on History and Society in Early Modern Europe* (Chicago, IL, 1979).

Houston, Robert, *Punishing the Dead? Suicide, Lordship, and Community in Britain, 1500–1830* (Oxford, 2010).

Hume, David, *The History of England: From the Invasion of Julius Caesar to the Revolution in 1688*, Vol. 5 (London, 1788).

Hume, David, *My Own Life*, ed. Iain Gordon Brown (Edinburgh, 2014).

Jeffery, Roger (ed.), *India in Edinburgh: 1750s to the Present* (Oxford, 2020).

Kaliamurthy, G., *Second Anglo-Mysore War (1780–84)* (New Delhi, 1987).

Kaul, C., *Media and the British Empire* (London, 2006).

Keating, Michael, 'The Strange Death of Unionist Scotland', *Government and Opposition*, vol. 45 (2010), pp. 365–85.

Kidd, Colin, *British Identities Before Nationalism: Ethnicity and Nationhood in the Atlantic World, 1600–1800* (Cambridge, 1999).

Kidd, Colin, *Union and Unionisms: Political Thought in Scotland, 1500–2000* (Cambridge, 2008)

Kirk, James (ed.), *Humanism and Reform: Essays in Honour of James K. Cameron* (Oxford, 1991).

Koditschek, Theodore, *Liberalism, Imperialism, and the Historical Imagination* (Cambridge, 2010).

Levitt, Ian, 'Britain, the Scottish Covenant Movement and Devolution, 1946–1950', *Scottish Affairs*, vol. 22 (1998), pp. 33–57.

MacCulloch, Dairmuid, 'The Change of Religion', in Collinson, Patrick (ed.), *The Sixteenth Century, 1485–1603* (Oxford, 2002), ch. 3.

MacDougal, Norman, *James IV* (Edinburgh, 1997).

MacGregor, Geddes, *The Thundering Scot* (Philadelphia, PA, 1957).

Mackenzie, John M. and Devine, T. M. (eds), *Scotland and the British Empire* (Oxford, 2011).

MacKillop, Andrew, *Emigrant Homecomings: The Return Movement of Migrants 1600–2000* (Manchester, 2005).

Marshall, P. J., *The Great Map of Mankind: British Perceptions of the World in the Age of Enlightenment* (London, 1982).

Marshall, P. J., *The Making and Unmaking of Empires: Britain, India and America c. 1750–1783* (Oxford, 2005).

Marshall, P. J., 'Imperial Britain', *Journal of Imperial and Commonwealth History*, vol. 23 (1995), pp. 379–94.

Mason, Roger and MacDougal, Norman (eds), *People and Power in Scotland* (Edinburgh, 1992).

Matthew, Colin (ed.), *The Nineteenth-Century: The British Isles 1815–1901* (Oxford, 2000).

Mayr, Ernst, 'When is Historiography Whiggish?', *Journal of History of Ideas*, vol. 51, no. 2 (1990), pp. 301–9.

McCarthy, A. and Mackenzie, J. M. (eds), *Global Migrations: The Scottish Diaspora since 1600* (Edinburgh, 2016).

McGilvary, George Kirk, *East India Patronage and the British State* (London, 2008).

Mitchell, James, *Devolution in the UK* (Edinburgh, 2009).

Mosman, George, *The Principal acts of the General Assembly of the Church of Scotland* (Edinburgh, 1821).

Musgrave, William, *Obituary Prior to 1800,* vols 44–45 (London, 1899).

Oakes, Henry, *An Authentic Narrative of the Treatment of the English, Who Were Taken Prisoners on the Reduction of Bednore* (London, 1785).

Paterson, Lindsay, *A Diverse Assembly* (Edinburgh, 1998).

Pearsall, Sarah, *Atlantic Families: Lives and Letters in the Later Eighteenth Century* (Oxford, 2008).

Pittock, Murray, *Scottish Nationality* (Basingstoke, 2001).

Razek, Rula, *Dress Codes: Reading Nineteenth-Century Fashion* (Stanford, CA, 1999).

Rorabacher, J, *Property, Land, Revenue, and Policy: The East India Company, C.1757–1825* (Oxford, 2016).

Ross, Ian Simpson, *The Life of Adam Smith* (Oxford, 2010).

Ross, Jamie, *James V* (Edinburgh, 1998).

Rothschild, Emma, *The Inner Life of Empire* (Princeton, NJ, 2011).

Rousseau, Jean-Jacques, *The Social Contract*, trans. H. J. Tozer (Ware, 1998).

Smith, Adam, *The Wealth of Nations* (Edinburgh, 1776).

Stewart, Gordon T., *Jute and Empire: The Calcutta Jute Wallahs and the Landscapes of Empire* (Manchester, 1998). Thorne, R., *The History of Parliament: the House of Commons 1790–1820* (London, 1986).

Vesey, Francis, *Reports of Cases Argued and Determined in the High Court of Chancery, from the Year M DCC LXXXIX to DCCC XVII* (Edinburgh, 1844).